"Our culture has become increasingly hostile to Christians. And our first instinct may be to avoid interacting with the world—especially when it comes to controversial issues. But Jesus said our faith is meant to be a public faith. So how can we engage positively with others on today's most divisive topics? That's what *When Culture Hates You* is all about. You'll find this a rich source of wisdom for knowing how to respond to opposition and discover a helpful variety of actions you can take to have a positive influence on today's culture."

—**Jack Hibbs**, president, Real Life Network; founding and senior pastor of Calvary Chapel Chino Hills, CA

"What Natasha Crain has accomplished in *When Culture Hates You* is remarkable. Her warning of the escalating dangers facing followers of Christ is appropriately charged with urgency—and not a moment too soon. A dark evil is rapidly descending on our children, our families, and our churches, and multitudes of Christians are oblivious to the threat.

"Crain's sobering analysis of current cultural deceptions is clearheaded, lucid, and completely faithful to a robust Christian worldview. Her book is also immensely practical with workable action guides and conversation helps provided for each issue she critiques.

"*When Culture Hates You* is precisely what Christians now need to be equipped to stand firm, to protect their families, and to resist the forces of darkness in this evil day."

—**Gregory Koukl**, president of Stand to Reason (str.org); author of *Tactics: A Game Plan for Discussing Your Christian Convictions* and *The Story of Reality: How the World Began, How It Ends, and Everything Important that Happens in Between*

"This book is clearheaded, well researched, and so needed! In these pages you will find answers to the many accusations hurled against Christians in our increasingly hostile culture. As I read it, I kept thinking to myself how well it balances Christian compassion with biblical authority and wisdom in its discussions of the controversies that swirl around in our families, churches, schools, and the media. Read it twice, then pass it on to a friend and ask them to do the same."

—**Erwin W. Lutzer**, pastor emeritus, Moody Church, Chicago

"In a post-truth culture, Christians are now finding themselves the objects of insults such as 'Christian nationalist,' and 'homophobic,' and 'oppressor.' If you find yourself confused by this new reality, *When Culture Hates You* will explain our current cultural ethos and give you practical action steps to live out your Christian values with courage and advocate for the common good. Don't let culture silence you. Let Natasha Crain help you live out your convictions in the public square with tenacity and grace."

—**Alisa Childers**, author of *Another Gospel?* and
host of *The Alisa Childers Podcast*

"How should Christians respond to a culture that's declared war on reality, reason, and biblical truth? *When Culture Hates You* has the answers. This timely book is a biblical guide to engaging a hostile culture with courage and conviction. It will help you to see just how important this fight is—and how engaging in it is not an abdication of our Christian duty to love, but a fulfillment of it. Every Christian who loves his neighbor and cares about our culture's decline needs to read this book."

—**Seth Dillon**, CEO of The Babylon Bee

"Ready or not, we as Christians are facing a growing number of cultural, social, and spiritual challenges. In this important book, Natasha Crain helps us get ready. With clear logic, biblical wisdom, and relentless relevance, she shows how we can be salt and light in this increasingly dark world, as Jesus commanded. Highly recommended."

—**Mark Mittelberg**, international speaker; author of *Contagious Faith*
and *The Questions Christians Hope No One Will Ask (With Answers)*

"The evangelical church now faces unprecedented challenges. In our secular age, we live in a society that is anti-Christian and has little tolerance for the historic faith of Christianity. The seductive culture has destabilized the thinking and discipleship of many inside the church. How do we live as salt and light in a hostile world? How do we seek shalom in the midst of modern-day Babylon? In this new book, Natasha Crain combines keen cultural analysis with biblical truth, developing a model of cultural engagement that is faithful to the gospel and filled with objective hope. Crain offers a timely and truthful call to the church in the twenty-first century."

—**Robert J. Pacienza**, senior pastor of Coral Ridge
Presbyterian Church, Fort Lauderdale, FL

"The Christian road is not an easy one. Knowing we're not alone as we navigate it is encouraging. Natasha's book offers clarity, guidance, and answers amidst the harsh political landscape that Christians must traverse. She tackles difficult subjects such as legislating morality, queer theory, social justice, Christian nationalism, and much more with courage and thoroughness, leaving no stone unturned. This book empowers Christians to remain steadfast when faced with harsh cultural opposition."

—**Melissa Dougherty**, content creator;
author of *Happy Lies*

"Jesus told us that the world would hate us as much as it hated Him. But He also promised that the gates of hell would not prevail against His church. Natasha Crain does an excellent job of helping us understand the challenges we face in today's post-Christian culture while at the same time giving us hope and confidence that, at the end of days, we win!"

—**Everett Piper**, president emeritus,
Oklahoma Wesleyan University

"Natasha Crain has done a wonderful service to the body of Christ by providing a needed introduction into Christian political theory. She explains a distinctly Christian approach to participate in the public square in everyday language."

—**Krista Bontrager**, coauthor, *Walking in Unity*;
vice president of Educational Programs and Biblical
Integrity at the Center for Biblical Unity

—**Monique Duson**, coauthor, *Walking in Unity*;
president, cofounder of Center for Biblical Unity

WHEN CULTURE HATES YOU

NATASHA CRAIN

HARVEST HOUSE PUBLISHERS
EUGENE. OREGON

All Scripture quotations are taken from the ESV® Bible (The Holy Bible, English Standard Version®), copyright © 2001 by Crossway, a publishing ministry of Good News Publishers. Used with permission. All rights reserved. The ESV text may not be quoted in any publication made available to the public by a Creative Commons license. The ESV may not be translated in whole or in part into any other language.

Published in association with the literary agency of Mark Sweeney & Associates.

Cover design by Faceout Studio, Molly von Borstel

Cover images © Nazario, image4stock / Shutterstock

Interior design by KUHN Design Group

For bulk, special sales, or ministry purchases, please call 1-800-547-8979.
Email: CustomerService@hhpbooks.com

M This logo is a federally registered trademark of the Hawkins Children's LLC. Harvest House Publishers, Inc., is the exclusive licensee of this trademark.

When Culture Hates You
Copyright © 2025 by Natasha Crain
Published by Harvest House Publishers
Eugene, Oregon 97408
www.harvesthousepublishers.com

ISBN 978-0-7369-8431-7 (pbk)
ISBN 978-0-7369-8432-4 (eBook)
ISBN 978-0-7369-9207-7 (eAudio)

Library of Congress Control Number: 2024935692

Printed in the United States of America

24 25 26 27 28 29 30 31 32 / BP / 10 9 8 7 6 5 4 3 2 1

*To my three kids: I pray you will grow up
to be bold lights in the darkness.*

ACKNOWLEDGMENTS

I'd like to thank Harvest House Publishers for being a committed partner in ministry. They are a rare example in Christian publishing of a company that is still committed to biblical truth in all the content they produce. I'm so grateful that they saw the value in the message of this book and have been enthusiastic at every point in moving it forward. Special thanks to president Bob Hawkins, whose commitment to the gospel and biblical fidelity drives the vision of the company; Sherrie Slopianka, whose marketing know-how and fun personality make every meeting enjoyable; and Becky Miller, who tirelessly works behind the scenes. Extra special thanks to my editor, Steve Miller, who is the most careful, thoughtful editor I can imagine having. He has truly been a partner in bringing this message to life.

I'd also like to thank Frank Turek for being willing to write the foreword and for his leading voice in calling Christians to engage faithfully in the public square. I'm inspired by his boldness and grateful to work with him.

And finally, my greatest thanks go to my husband, Bryan. I could not do any of the things I do in ministry without his continual support. He is endlessly patient with my deadlines and cheers me on because he deeply believes in the value of this work. Thank you, Bryan, for your generous love and support.

CONTENTS

■ ■ ■

Foreword by Frank Turek 11

PART 1: UNDERSTANDING THE HATE

1. Jesus Said It Would Happen 17

*"If the world hates you, know that it has hated me before
it hated you" (John 15:18).*

2. God Defines the Common Good 35

*The definition of good isn't up for debate…as much as
culture may think it is.*

3. When the Common Good Is Political 53

*Advocating for the common good out of our love for others
sometimes includes the political.*

4. Should Christians Impose Their Views on Others? 71

And four other objections to public Christian influence

5. Persevering in the Public Square 89

*Know your (biblical) **A**uthority, strengthen **C**onviction,
and maintain **T**enacity (ACT).*

PART 2: RESPONDING TO AND PERSEVERING THROUGH TODAY'S MOST PROMINENT CHARGES

6. Dangerous Christian Nationalists 111

The View from the Mainstream Media

7. Power-Hungry Oppressors 135
    The View from Secular Social Justice Activists

8. Controlling Misogynists 157
    The View from Pro-Choice Activists

9. Cruel Rights-Deniers 181
    The View from Transgender Activists

10. Hateful Bigots 207
    The View from the Sexual Revolution

Epilogue: Letting Your Light Shine in Spite of Hate 233
    "Take no part in the unfruitful works of darkness,
    but instead expose them" (Ephesians 5:11).

Recommendations for Further Study 237

Notes 243

FOREWORD

Frank Turek

Before I became a full-time speaker and a writer, I conducted leadership training for Fortune 500 companies. One such company was CISCO. Another was Bank of America. Both of them fired me in 2011—not because my job performance was poor, but because an employee in my training program discovered I had written a book called *Correct, Not Politically Correct*. My sin? I had defended the biblical view of marriage.

After writing to the chairman of CISCO, I was referred to the head of inclusion, tolerance, and diversity for an explanation. I asked her, "If you're all about inclusion, tolerance, and diversity, then why was I excluded and not tolerated for holding a diverse view?" She couldn't give me a coherent answer because there isn't one. In fact, if irony could kill, she would have died right there!

The real answer is that *inclusion, tolerance,* and *diversity* are words that have been redefined to mean something completely different than what they originally meant. Now they mean, "If you don't believe in the new cultural values that directly contradict the Bible and common sense, you will be excluded and not tolerated."

After going public with what both companies did, I knew I'd be too radioactive to work in "tolerant" corporate America again. Thankfully, I had a fallback position and began doing speaking and writing full time with CrossExamined.org.

But what about you? Are you ever afraid to say or post the biblical view of a moral issue? Worried that to do so might cost you your job? Do you feel the need to censor yourself to avoid conflict? Have you started to tell people—even your closest friends and relatives—what they want to hear rather than what they need to hear? Have you unwittingly bought into the cultural lie that love requires approval?

Where can you get help to navigate the minefield America has become?

Thankfully, the Seventh Fleet has arrived, and her name is Natasha Crain. I've been blessed to work alongside Natasha for about a decade, and I can say that her insights into engaging a hostile culture are powerful and practical.

For example, in her book that preceded this one, *Faithfully Different*, Natasha revealed how modern secular people tend to think about life and how to live it. They believe that *feelings* are the ultimate guide, *happiness* is the ultimate goal, *judging* is the ultimate sin, and *God* is the ultimate guess.

Who are you, Christian, to judge my actions because I'm just following my feelings toward happiness? I need to follow my heart! And don't impose your God's morality on me because no one is sure if he or she really exists anyway.

You've probably heard some or all of that. In fact, if you think about the people in your life who are not "religious"—and maybe even some who claim to be Christians—they follow that same "me-centered" approach Natasha revealed in *Faithfully Different*, don't they? Their theology is really *me*-ology set "to suit their own passions" (2 Timothy 4:3). The question is, how do you best interact with such people to accomplish both the great commission and the cultural commission?

When Culture Hates You shows you how. Natasha delves into the hottest topics that, regrettably, many pastors are reluctant to address, including transgenderism, critical race theory, social justice, charges of Christian nationalism, the taking of unborn lives, the loss of the freedom to live out the Christian faith, and an absolutely shocking chapter on the sexual "liberation" of children.

Along the way, Natasha gives you very practical action steps at the end of each chapter, which are designed to help you advance the cause of Christ. But before she does that, she shows why the culture hates us and answers many objections people have when they claim Christians are "imposing their views on others."

When people make that objection, as Natasha will point out, they are doing exactly what they're complaining about—"imposing *their* views on others." Whether it's in a personal relationship, a business, or a country, the rules and laws that are established are an imposition of *someone's* morality. In fact, all rules and laws legislate someone's morality. The only question is, whose morality should be legislated?

If you haven't noticed, new moralities and rights are invented about every ten minutes in America. Quite often, the people advocating for these new rights are atheists who claim you are wrong for not celebrating their new rights. You should ask them, "By what moral standard are you claiming those rights? Unless God exists, there is no objective moral standard, and, therefore, there are no rights." In effect, these people are attempting to steal objective morality from God while claiming He doesn't exist.

Nearly every page of this brilliant book exposes fallacies like this. And while Natasha certainly makes the case that Christians must love their neighbors by ensuring good laws are passed, this is not a book primarily about politics. It is much broader than that. This is a book about discipleship. It shows that we Christians ought to be ambassadors for Christ in *every* area of our lives—not just at church, but at home, at work, at play, online, in our local communities, and in our country.

Yes, the culture is dark and hates us, but remember what Jesus said our response should be: "You are the light of the world. A city set on a hill cannot be hidden. Nor do people light a lamp and put it under a basket, but on a stand, and it gives light to all in the house. In the same way, let your light shine before others, so that they may see your good works and give glory to your Father who is in heaven" (Matthew 5:14-16).

You're not doing that if fear is keeping you silent. Read on to see how you can make your light shine.

Frank Turek

PART 1:

UNDERSTANDING THE HATE

JESUS SAID IT WOULD HAPPEN

*If the world hates you, know that it has
hated me before it hated you.*

JOHN 15:18

■ ■ ■

On March 26, 1997, sheriff's deputies received an anonymous call to conduct a welfare check at a mansion in Rancho Santa Fe, California. When they responded, they found a shocking scene: Thirty-nine people were dead in what turned out to be the largest mass suicide in United States history.

But it wasn't just the scale of the event that made headlines. The deceased were also mysteriously dressed in identical black tracksuits and brand-new Nike shoes. Each person had the same cropped haircut, and a large purple cloth covered each of the bodies.

News of the bizarre scene spread quickly, and the media flooded in. It was eventually discovered that the group had ingested a fatal mix of applesauce, sedatives, and vodka in order to facilitate a collective suicide. Why? They thought they needed to shed their earthly bodies in order to board an alien spacecraft hidden behind an approaching comet—a spacecraft that would pass them through "Heaven's Gate" and into a higher existence.

People were enthralled with the Heaven's Gate cult. Despite the morbid nature of what happened, the group became the subject of endless jokes. Even *Saturday Night Live* made a parody about them. Culture clearly thought the people in this cult were delusional and outlandishly wrong.

But culture didn't *hate* them.

When your doorbell rings and you discover two well-dressed people from a local church standing on your doorstep, there's a good possibility that they're Jehovah's Witnesses. Well known to the world for their door-to-door preaching, Jehovah's Witnesses reportedly send more than 8.5 million people into neighborhoods each year.

The internet abounds with humorous memes of people desperately searching for a way to escape from these evangelists on their doorstep. Apparently, if you've ever looked through your peephole and quietly tiptoed back into your house hoping your unsolicited church visitors won't ring again, you're not alone. Culture widely considers Jehovah's Witnesses to be annoyingly persistent in their door-to-door activities.

But culture doesn't *hate* them.

If you drive through parts of Lancaster County, Pennsylvania, you'll probably have to slow down to accommodate horses and buggies driven by men dressed in black broad-brimmed or straw hats. As you pass through that rural countryside, it may look like a scene from another century. But it's just everyday life for the local Amish community.

Lancaster County is home to the largest and most well-known settlement of Amish in America, though there are more than 350,000 Amish living in 32 states. Known for shunning modern conveniences like cars, the Amish form close-knit communities dedicated to simple living in pursuit of an undistracted devotion to God. Millions of people flock to Amish country each year to get a glimpse of their unique way of life. At the same time, the Amish are often criticized for being backward and isolated. Culture certainly thinks they're a curiosity.

But culture doesn't *hate* them.

There's a reason culture doesn't hate these three groups, even when it's had an otherwise negative assessment of them: *These groups haven't attempted to influence the public square with their contrarian views.*

The *public square* is anywhere views are shared for the purpose of shaping public opinion on how society should function. If contrarian groups keep to themselves such that culture can forge ahead in the absence of any perceived imposition of beliefs from those groups, they're in the clear. Go ahead and don matching tracksuits with your friends in anticipation of an alien ship, spend your free time knocking on doors, or live like it's 1750. Culture might think you're pitiable, annoying, or weird, but it won't hate you.

That level of bitter resentment is reserved for groups who believe they *shouldn't* keep their contrarian views to themselves. Groups whose very purpose includes a charge to influence the culture around them based on beliefs starkly opposed to those cherished by that culture.

Groups…like Christians.

Who Is *Culture*?

When I say that culture does or does not hate certain groups, you probably have a general idea of what I mean by *culture*. But because that word can imply some very different things in different contexts, it's important to clarify what I mean by it for the purposes of this book.

In the broadest sense, culture refers to the way of life for a society—the manners, dress, language, religion, arts, and customs generally shared by a group of people at a given time. That's the kind of definition you'd find in a dictionary. But in everyday conversation, people typically use the word *culture* to mean something much more nuanced. Culture, in this colloquial sense, is personified. *It refers to the people and institutions who hold the values considered to be in vogue for a given society.*

For example, if someone says to you, "Today's culture thinks that…," you intuitively know how the sentence might end given what you observe around you. Any of the following statements would readily fit the presumed context: love means affirmation; it's better to be spiritual than religious; happiness is the goal of life; you shouldn't be judgmental; or any number of other prevalent ideas.

This zeitgeist, or "spirit of the times," can be observed at both individual and institutional levels. Examples of key cultural institutions would include the media, entertainment, government, and academia. Individuals influence those institutions, and those institutions, in turn, influence more individuals. That cycle is ongoing and mutually reinforcing, leading over time to certain values becoming culturally acceptable or celebrated and others becoming anathema. Culture, then, is a snapshot of the current state of society's values.

That said, it's important to also emphasize some qualifications about what *isn't* implied by my use of the term *culture* in this book.

First, saying culture thinks or does something is not making a statement about the thoughts or actions of all cultures at all times. For example, the Amish were persecuted by their culture in times past, but that cultural hatred no longer persists. The term *culture* necessarily implies a context of time and place.

Second, saying culture thinks or does something is not to suggest that every single person in a given society thinks or does the same. We can broadly say culture doesn't hate the Amish, for example, while recognizing that there are surely some people who do (particularly if they've had a bad personal experience with the Amish community).

Third, saying culture thinks or does something is not making a claim about the percent of people in a given society who think or do the same; it's impossible to broadly quantify the spirit of the times when that encompasses constantly shifting and diverse factors. But even if you *could* quantify it, sheer numbers wouldn't necessarily tell the full story. When a statistical minority is more aggressive in influencing the public square with their values than a statistical majority that holds opposing views, it's the minority's values that will often come to define the culture.

In summary, for the purposes of this book, culture refers to the people and institutions who hold the values widely considered to be accepted and celebrated in the United States today.[1]

Beyond the Soup Kitchen

The significance of culture to Christians cannot be overstated, because culture functions as a gatekeeper of the ideas that fashionable society deems admissible to the public square at any given time. And if you're a group whose values have become anathema, the gatekeepers won't merely roll a condescending eye at you and then let you in. They'll funnel their hatred of your contrarian values into an active campaign to keep your influence out.

It's probably not news to you that this is increasingly the relationship between culture and Christians today.

It's worth noting, however, that culture doesn't necessarily hate everything Christians might advocate for in the public square. For example, people with all kinds of different views about the world would agree that it's a good thing to volunteer at or donate to local soup kitchens. If you're part of a Christian group passionate about that form of service, you might decide to publicly advocate for the cause in some way. In doing so, it's likely that no one will hate you, even if they disagree on the best way to approach the issue of food insecurity. Serving food to those in need is an action still widely considered to be a moral good.

But now let's say you're a group who believes humans in the womb have the same value and God-given right to life as humans who have already been born, and you decide to publicly advocate for a local pro-life pregnancy center.

I don't have to tell you we're out of soup kitchen territory now.

In today's culture, the pro-life position is seen as a repulsive injustice to women. Consequently, culture doesn't think that those who hold such a position are merely mistaken—a belief akin to thinking an alien ship is coming—it thinks they're *oppressors*. If you speak or act publicly against abortion, you'll be morally condemned and detested for being harmful, oppressive, cruel, toxic, violent, or misogynistic (more on that in chapter 8).

Loving your neighbor by publicly advocating for a soup kitchen and loving your neighbor by publicly advocating for the protection of life in the womb are both outworkings of a biblical worldview. But, as we just saw, there's a major difference in how those two actions are perceived by culture. The former will likely draw ambivalence or approval, the latter serious condemnation. As Christians, therefore, we aren't resented for *everything* we believe and do, but because we're reviled for opposing some of the values most cherished by culture, we're increasingly hated as a group.

The gatekeepers would love nothing more than for us to just keep serving soup while being silent about the issues on which we're at odds with culture—and that's a tempting proposition for many Christians. After all, if we did that, culture would like us (or at least like us more). Who wants to be hated?

But being hated is exactly what Jesus told us to expect if we're going to follow His commands. Silence in exchange for cultural respect is a deal with the devil.

Jesus Said It Would Happen

Knowing what the Bible says about culture hating the followers of Jesus is the key to understanding the moment we're in, so let's go to Scripture.

Jesus called His 12 disciples together one day to prepare them to go out on a mission. He gave them the authority to cast out unclean spirits and to heal every disease and affliction (Matthew 10:1). He then instructed them at length on what to expect and do on their journey. It certainly wasn't a talk designed to encourage the disciples with any idea that the mission field would warmly embrace them. Jesus warned that they'd be handed over to local councils and be flogged in the synagogues (Matthew 10:17), that family members would betray each other and have one another put to death (Matthew 10:21), and that He didn't come to bring peace, but a sword (Matthew 10:34). It's within that context that Jesus said the following: "You will be hated by all for my name's sake. But the one who endures to the end will be saved" (Matthew 10:22). Later, in Matthew 24:9, Jesus repeated to His disciples, "You will be hated by all nations for my name's sake."

These verses should raise the question of *why* Jesus's disciples would be hated. In the immediate context of these passages, Jesus doesn't explicitly say why. But we get a more detailed picture of what He had in mind in His words from John 15:18-21:

> If the world hates you, know that it has hated me before it hated you. If you were of the world, the world would love you as its own; but because you are not of the world, but I chose you out of the world, therefore the world hates you. Remember the word that I said to you: "A servant is not greater than his master." If they persecuted me, they will also persecute you. If they kept my word, they will also keep yours. But all these things they will do to you on account of my name, because they do not know him who sent me.

Now we have the explanation: If the disciples were *of the world*, the world would have loved them as its own, but because they *weren't* of the world, the world would hate them. Jesus similarly connected this explanation when He prayed, "I have given them your word, and the world has hated them because they are not of the world, just as I am not of the world" (John 17:14).

So what does it mean to be of the world? The Greek word translated "world" here is *kosmos*. *Kosmos* in this context refers to unbelieving mankind, which is governed by evil. To say that unbelievers are governed by evil isn't a hyperbolic theological claim. Jesus bluntly said on multiple occasions that Satan is the ruler of the *kosmos* (John 12:31; 14:30; 16:11). In fact, He told a crowd of Jews who claimed to be children of God through their physical descent from Abraham that they were actually children of Satan (John 8:44)! Why? He said it was because *their will was to do the devil's desires.*

That's the pivotal distinction. People are either children of Satan or children of God. People who are "of the world" are children of Satan, and, under his influence, desire to go their own way rather than God's way. In Ephesians 2:1-3, Paul says all of us have that desire for self-rule by nature:

> You were dead in the trespasses and sins in which you once walked, following the course of this world, following the prince of the power of the air, the spirit that is now at work in the sons of disobedience—among whom we all once lived in the passions of our flesh, carrying out the desires of the body and the mind, and were by nature children of wrath, like the rest of mankind.

Those who remain of the world are *slaves to sin* because they remain in rebellion to their Creator; in following their own passions and desires, they do the will of Satan. Those who give their lives to Jesus, however, receive a new nature and are a new creation (2 Corinthians 5:17). They become children of God (John 1:12) and are now *slaves to righteousness.* Paul emphasizes this contrast in Romans 6:16-18:

> Do you not know that if you present yourselves to anyone as obedient slaves, you are slaves of the one whom you

obey, either of sin, which leads to death, or of obedience, which leads to righteousness? But thanks be to God, that you who were once slaves of sin have become obedient from the heart to the standard of teaching to which you were committed, and, having been set free from sin, have become slaves of righteousness.

So let's recap. Jesus said the world would hate His disciples because they were not *of* the world; if they *were* of the world, the world would love them as its own. To be of the world means to be under the governing influence of Satan, resulting in being a slave to sin. Conversely, to be a child of God is to be a slave to righteousness.

That leads to our final question: Why do the children of Satan necessarily hate the children of God? John addresses this question directly in 1 John 3:9-13:

No one born of God makes a practice of sinning, for God's seed abides in him; and he cannot keep on sinning, because he has been born of God. By this it is evident who are the children of God, and who are the children of the devil: whoever does not practice righteousness is not of God, nor is the one who does not love his brother. For this is the message that you have heard from the beginning, that we should love one another. We should not be like Cain, who was of the evil one and murdered his brother. And why did he murder him? Because his own deeds were evil and his brother's righteous. Do not be surprised, brothers, that the world hates you.

In short, the children of God will be hated because they practice righteousness and the children of Satan practice evil.

Righteousness is despised by a fallen world.

When the children of God practice righteousness, they shine light on the works of the world, unveiling the truth of what they are: evil. Satan may masquerade as an angel of light (2 Corinthians 11:14), but that illusion is shattered by the true light that comes from the followers of Jesus. *Of course* those who are of the world will hate that. And they'll hate *you* for making it happen.

Christianity Is a Public Faith

Given that this is why Jesus said the world would hate His disciples, it follows that He presumed they would be engaging with the world in some way; where evil continues in darkness, there's no light to hate. Being a Christian, therefore, doesn't end with a private profession of faith in Jesus as Lord and Savior. If we profess that Jesus is Lord over our lives, we'll live in obedience to His commands (John 14:15)—commands that include the public engagement necessary to make disciples of all nations (Matthew 28:19-20) and to advocate for righteousness in our given cultures. Jesus spoke of this latter role in His famous Sermon on the Mount words about being salt and light (Matthew 5:13-16):

> You are the salt of the earth, but if salt has lost its taste, how shall its saltiness be restored? It is no longer good for anything except to be thrown out and trampled under people's feet.

> You are the light of the world. A city set on a hill cannot be hidden. Nor do people light a lamp and put it under a basket, but on a stand, and it gives light to all in the house. In the same way, let your light shine before others, so that they may see your good works and give glory to your Father who is in heaven.

As salt, we preserve a world that would otherwise be entirely under the destructive rule of Satan and enslaved to sin. We preserve the world for enough time that God's purposes can be worked out. As light, we expose the darkness for what it is and bring glory to God in the process (see also John 3:19-21; 8:12; Ephesians 5:11). These roles of preserving and exposing are inherently of a public nature. *They require Christians to advocate for righteousness in the public square.* We aren't preserving or exposing anything by sitting passively in our living rooms.

It's at this point that some Christians get squeamish. They agree that we're to be salt and light, but they believe that should only include sharing the gospel and doing good works in one's private life—not advocating for righteousness in how society functions. In response, four points should be made.

First, acknowledging the need to advocate for righteousness in how society functions doesn't imply there isn't *also* a need for Christians to share the gospel and do good works in their private lives. We can share the gospel, do good works in our private lives, *and* advocate for righteousness in how society functions. This should be a rather obvious point, but it warrants an explicit remark because it's a common reason Christians give for avoiding the public square. The underlying sentiment is that our primary mission is to share the gospel and do good works, so time spent on social issues is a distraction from what we should *really* be doing. While it's a worthwhile warning to not turn our mission into a purely earthly one, the possibility of Christians erring in that direction is not an argument for not caring about the righteous functioning of society at all. The laws passed by our society affect our ability to even preach the gospel in the first place.

Second, the gospel itself implies the need to care about how society functions and act accordingly. When Christians say we should "just" preach the gospel, it's worth asking what they believe the gospel is. The gospel is the good news that God loved the world so much, He gave His only Son to die as payment for our sins so we could be reconciled to Him and have everlasting life. When we respond to this gracious offer of salvation, we submit to Jesus as Lord and follow His commands out of our love for Him. *Caring about the way in which society functions is just one part of following Jesus's second greatest commandment, to "love your neighbor as yourself" (Matthew 22:36-40).* Part of loving your neighbor is caring about the quality of their lives in the context of the society in which they live. Put simply, we should want God's best for them.

Third, when we care about the quality of people's lives in the context of the society in which they live, we should want God's best for them regardless of how many people are responsive to the gospel message at any given time. Christians sometimes believe that the extent of societal transformation for which we're responsible is preaching the gospel so that individual consciences will be transformed and more individuals will then make righteous choices. But when you apply that logic to specific cases in history, few people would maintain the same position consistently. For example, imagine someone saying the following: "I think Christians in the nineteenth century really messed up by working to abolish slavery. They should have just preached the gospel so that individual lives would be transformed, and over time, that would have changed society to the point it would no longer find slavery morally acceptable." I'm guessing nearly every reader would instinctively disagree with this imaginary person, but take a moment to consider why. Four million enslaved people were set free by the Emancipation Proclamation in 1863. How many more years would people have had to suffer in slavery if Christians had simply waited for a critical mass of Americans to have their moral sensibilities transformed through personal salvation? What if that critical mass was *never* reached? Should slavery have continued? Of course not. Fortunately, there were Christians at the time who recognized the need to shine light on the deeds of darkness and advocate for righteousness—the end to a wicked institution. They preached the gospel, but they didn't wait to see how many conversions would happen before working to bring an end to societal evil.

Finally, God's concern for how society functions runs throughout the Bible. It's clear that God cares both about individual relationships with Him *and* the moral health of the societies in which individuals live. The following are just a few notable examples where biblical people were exhorted to proactively shape societies that function in a righteous way:

- In Isaiah chapter 1, God expresses His wrath toward the people of Judah for their sins and empty religious ceremonies. He presses them to cease doing evil and instead "learn to do good; seek justice, correct oppression; bring justice to the fatherless, plead the widow's cause" (vv. 16-17; see also Zechariah 7:10). This, of course, would require public engagement and advocacy.

- In the Jewish exile to pagan Babylon, the prophet Daniel was an official in King Nebuchadnezzar's court. Daniel told the king, "Break off your sins by practicing righteousness, and your iniquities by showing mercy to the oppressed, that there may perhaps be a lengthening of your prosperity" (Daniel 4:27). Here we see that God expected even pagan societies to function in a righteous way (see also Amos 1–2 and Obadiah).

- God told the Jewish exiles in Babylon, "Seek the welfare of the city where I have sent you into exile, and pray to the Lord on its behalf, for in its welfare you will find your welfare" (Jeremiah 29:7). God didn't want the exiles to thumb their noses at the pagan culture in which they were forced to live. They were to seek what was best for the culture—which would be to everyone's benefit, including their own.

- John the Baptist was thrown into prison because he had rebuked the civil leader Herod Antipas for marrying his brother's wife and "for all the evil things that Herod had done" (Luke 3:19-20). Presumably, those evil actions included what Herod had done in his governing capacity.

Being salt and light isn't *only* about having a godly influence on culture, but biblical examples demonstrate it certainly includes that.

When Culture Hates You

Something that's easy to gloss over in Jesus's words about being salt and light is how that passage ends: "Let your light shine before others, *so that they may see your good works and give glory to your Father who is in heaven*" (Matthew 5:16, emphasis added). This is a seemingly surprising conclusion given our earlier discussion about being hated for righteousness. In fact, it's a jarring contrast even against Jesus's immediately preceding words (Matthew 5:10-12):

> Blessed are those who are persecuted for righteousness' sake, for theirs is the kingdom of heaven.

> Blessed are you when others revile you and persecute you and utter all kinds of evil against you falsely on my account. Rejoice and be glad, for your reward is great in heaven, for so they persecuted the prophets who were before you.

So which is it? Will the world hate us for shining light, or will it see our good works and glorify God?

The answer is both.

Sometimes when we as Christians testify to righteousness through our words and actions, people will have their eyes opened and glorify God as the source of all that is good and true. Praise the Lord for those times!

But in other circumstances, Christians will be reviled and even persecuted. Yes, Jesus said that we would be blessed when that happens, but that doesn't mean it's easy. The prophet Jeremiah spoke God's truth to his culture, but he also lamented, "I have become a laughingstock all the day; everyone mocks me. For whenever I speak, I cry out, I shout, 'Violence and destruction!' For the word of the Lord has become for me a reproach and derision all day long" (Jeremiah 20:7-8). Jeremiah wasn't an exception. The pattern of the Bible is that all the prophets suffered in some way (Acts 7:52). It's never been popular to publicly advocate for righteousness in a fallen world.

No book is needed to equip and encourage Christians to persevere through cultural hatred when publicly advocating for something like a soup kitchen. As we discussed, no one will hate you for that.

But *when* culture hates you—*when* you're reviled for promoting your views in the public square—it takes deep conviction and courage to nonetheless persevere for the common good. That requires biblical, cultural, and civic understanding that Christians don't necessarily have by default. And therein lies the purpose of this book: to give Christ followers the crucial understanding required to confidently advocate for righteousness in today's increasingly dark and hostile culture.

Part 1 will establish important foundational principles on the nature of Christian public influence. The purpose of this section is to provide readers with a framework for evaluating *any* common-good issue, whether it's one we address specifically in part 2 or not. So don't skip part 1! It functions as far more than a lead-in to part 2. It's relevant to a plethora of issues Christians encounter beyond the specific ones we'll consider in this book.

That said, in part 2, we'll apply our understanding from part 1 to five issues that are of especially great significance for the common good today—issues on which Christians are also at great odds with culture and receive significant condemnation accordingly. These aren't the only issues drawing resentment against Christians, but they represent a selection of those on which Christians most urgently need clarity.

I pray that *When Culture Hates You* will equip and encourage you to be the light God wants you to be in this world.

CHAPTER 1 SUMMARY

- Culture, in the context of this book, refers to the people and institutions who hold the values widely considered to be accepted and celebrated in the United States today.

- Culture hates groups who seek to influence the public square with contrarian values—groups like Christians.

- Being hated shouldn't surprise us. Jesus taught that the world would hate His disciples because they were not *of* the world. To be *of* the world means to be under the governing influence of Satan, resulting in being a slave to sin.

- Those who are of the world—children of Satan—naturally hate the children of God for practicing righteousness because their righteousness reveals the works of the world to be evil.

- The Christian "salt and light" roles of preserving and exposing are inherently of a public nature. They require us to advocate for righteousness in the public square, even when we're hated for it.

CHAPTER 2

GOD DEFINES THE COMMON GOOD

The definition of good isn't up for debate...
as much as culture may think it is.

■ ■ ■

At the end of chapter 1, I wrote that it takes deep conviction and courage to persevere for the common good in a hostile culture. That was the first time I used the term *common good* in this book, but you likely didn't pause and scratch your head over what I meant. On the surface, it seems relatively self-explanatory. Yet, as we'll see in this chapter, the meaning requires far more reflection than you might imagine before we can appropriately understand what, exactly, Christians should be persevering for in the public square.

The idea of the common good has a lengthy history in philosophy, theology, political science, and economics, reaching as far back as Aristotle and Plato in ancient Greece. My use of the term in this book is not intended to import anything in particular from those contexts. Rather, I use it more simply to refer to "the set of conditions in society, or a state of affairs in society, where all of the various constituencies and elements of society are able to thrive."[1]

The *common* part of the term, then, refers to the relational nature of society. There are 7.9 billion people who live on Earth today, and we obviously don't live in 7.9 billion individual silos. We necessarily live in relationship with other people through communities of various types and sizes. The life we share in common in those contexts—whether we're talking about a local neighborhood or an entire nation—requires us to establish and agree to certain parameters within which community life will take place. The common *good*, then, refers to the conditions and parameters that allow those in a given community to thrive. Note that this is something we presumably all want; you would be hard-pressed to find someone who *doesn't* want their communities to thrive. In fact, we diagnose those who have no regard for the well-being of society with a mental illness called antisocial personality disorder. We assume that humans who have healthy cognitive functioning share a desire for what we would broadly call the common good.

On a cursory level, therefore, the phrase *common good* is pretty simple to understand. The word *common* refers to the shared life humans have in a given community context, and the word *good* refers to the thriving that humans normally wish for their communities to attain. Yet, as we'll see in this book, *the vast majority of culture wars today are over the common good.* By and large, those wars aren't happening because some people want what's good for society and others don't. They're happening because people disagree on *what* is good for society.

This is where the concept of the common good must get far more nuanced.

Imagine, for example, putting a group of ten five-year-olds in a classroom and telling them to form a new tiny country just for themselves. You ask them to create three key rules that they'll live by, and you specify that those rules need to be good for their community. You give them 30 minutes and then return to hear what they've established. If you've ever spent much time around kids of that age, you wouldn't be surprised to come back to the following three rules for the common good of this new kindergarten kingdom:

1. Cookies will be served for breakfast, lunch, and dinner daily.

2. Cartoons will replace classroom instruction.

3. No one will ever be asked to pick up their own toys.

As an adult returning to this classroom, you would probably chuckle at the naivety of kids thinking these rules are for their good. Despite their perception of what is good, living this way would lead to some objectively bad consequences: malnutrition, lack of education, and a physically hazardous environment covered in Legos (the most painful thing on Earth to step on, as every parent can attest). Just because a person thinks something is good doesn't mean it actually is.

In this illustration, the kids would disagree with adults on what is for their common good because they lack certain types of knowledge and experience. But knowledge and experience alone don't account for the different ways in which people define good; if they did, we would see far more agreement among adults with similar backgrounds. We don't see that widespread agreement, however, because a person's definition of good is ultimately rooted in something much deeper and more complex—their worldview.

Why Do People Disagree on What's Good?

A worldview is a set of beliefs about the fundamental nature of reality. Every human capable of holding beliefs has a worldview whether they've consciously arrived at those beliefs or not. Our worldview is formed by how we answer questions such as where humans came from, who we are, why we're here, how we should live, and what happens after we die. In short, our worldview is the lens through which we see *everything*.

When we consider the dictionary definition of *good*, we can see why it's a concept that's inherently connected to people's worldview and why there are consequently so many ideas of good competing in culture. Good is defined as that which is 1) morally right or 2) beneficial to someone or something. Let's look at each of these senses of the word *good* in the context of worldview questions.

Good as Morally Right

A person's view of what, if anything, is morally right or wrong is intrinsically tied to worldview questions because the determination of those moral categories depends on what you use as your standard. For example, if you're learning to play a piano piece by Mozart, the standard by which your notes can be judged as right or wrong is the music he wrote. You might not like the way in which he wrote it, but if you start playing notes according to your own preferences, an observer can objectively say you're playing *wrong* notes relative to the standard of the original piece. But if you sit down at a piano to play your own creation—*not* an existing piece—there's no standard against which your notes can be judged. The standard is effectively your own preferences because in this case, no external standard exists.

In a similar way, if God doesn't exist and humans are merely the product of blind evolutionary forces over billions of years, there can be no objective *moral* standard against which our actions can be judged. That's because there would be no higher-than-human moral authority with the ability and right to impose a moral law on all people telling us what we should or shouldn't do. And, as such, no human would be in an authoritative position to claim that *anything* is right or wrong for all people; right and wrong would simply be a matter of individual preference. If I were to advocate for the common good while holding this as my worldview—and be logically consistent—I would need to recognize that everyone's idea of what is morally right or wrong is equally legitimate. The best I could do is gain enough power to impose *my* idea of good on everyone else. There would be no objective moral good transcending people's opinions to which I could appeal.

Let's consider a second worldview scenario and again see how a person's definition of good would depend on the nature of that reality. What if a creator God existed but never revealed Himself or His moral law through some kind of Scripture or other means? What, in that case, would be morally right or wrong? We would have no way of knowing, because in this scenario, the Creator didn't tell us! One human might believe that it's morally right to marry ten people, while another might believe it's morally right to marry only one. But neither could appeal to an objective definition of good that applies to all people because this God never made His moral standards known. Thus, the end result is actually the same as in the last scenario: If I were to advocate for the common good while holding this as my worldview—and be logically consistent—I would need to recognize that everyone's idea of what is morally right or wrong is equally legitimate. In the last worldview scenario, that was because God didn't exist, so objective moral rights and wrongs couldn't exist either. In this scenario, objective moral rights and wrongs *could* exist given the existence of a being with the ability and authority to set moral standards, but we wouldn't have any way of *knowing* if they did and what they were if He never revealed those things. Defining the common good would be anyone's guess.

Let's consider a final scenario. What if a creator God existed *and* chose to reveal His moral will and requirements for all of humanity through some kind of Scripture—say, the Bible, the Quran, or the Book of Mormon? This scenario about reality has very different implications. In this case, humans would have an objective basis for knowing the moral standards that exist and what they are—moral standards that apply to everyone. Like playing a piece by Mozart, you could, in this world, make choices that are morally right or wrong relative to an objective standard that exists external to your moral preferences. If I were to advocate for the common good while holding this as my worldview—and be logically consistent—I would recognize that the good I seek must be in accordance with God's objective standards and that people who seek the common good according to standards that conflict with those of God are advocating for things that are *not actually good*, no matter how well-intentioned they may be.

We could continue to flesh out the implications for the common good across a variety of other possible realities, but these three scenarios should suffice to demonstrate the key point here: The existence and definition of moral goods inherently depend on the nature of the universe in which we live. As a result, if people disagree about what kind of universe we live in and/or are logically inconsistent in applying their worldview to matters of morality, they'll disagree over how to define the common (moral) good.

Good as Beneficial

The second sense of the word *good* that's relevant to our discussion is when something is beneficial. To be beneficial is to produce a good outcome *relative to a purpose*. If I asked you, "Should I hit this with a hammer?," your response would naturally be, "What is it you want to hit?" That's because we intuitively recognize that an action can be either beneficial (good) or harmful (bad), depending on the purpose of the object. Hitting a nail with a hammer produces a good outcome because the purpose of a nail is to go into a wall. But hitting a fragile toy with a hammer produces a bad outcome because the purpose of the toy is to entertain a child. Hitting it with a hammer would destroy its ability to fulfill that purpose.

In order to know whether something benefits a person or group of people, we therefore have to know what the purpose of a human is. And that, again, depends on the nature of the universe in which we live. Let's see why by considering sample scenarios about reality once more. Because the logic is similar to that of the preceding discussion, we'll look at just two scenarios this time and keep them brief.

In the first scenario, there is no God, and people are merely the physical products of blind evolutionary chance. We're essentially accidents with no purpose. In such a world, people would not exist "for" anything. Anyone could dub any action beneficial according to their subjective definition of human purpose. For example, a person could claim that killing their depressed neighbor was beneficial for that neighbor because it eliminated his suffering. If the depressed neighbor didn't exist for any objective purpose, who would have the authority to say otherwise? If his self-defined purpose was to live with minimal suffering, ending his life would be beneficial relative to that purpose.

But consider another scenario. What if there's a God who created people with a specific purpose—say, for example, to know and live in relationship with Him until the time when He decides each human's life is complete? And what if He revealed that purpose in a way that all people could know it? In the case of the depressed neighbor, there would now be someone with the authority to say that taking his life would actually *not* benefit him: God. No matter how convinced the depressed neighbor might be that it would benefit him to die, he would be objectively wrong. In this scenario, taking his life would be harmful relative to his God-given purpose.

As we can see, the determination of whether an action is beneficial or harmful inherently depends on the nature of the universe in which we live, just as the existence and definition of what is morally good does. And, once again, if people disagree about what kind of universe we live in and/or are logically inconsistent in applying their worldview to these questions, they will disagree over what is beneficial or harmful for people when advocating for the common good.

People may have all kinds of views about reality, leading to cultural wars over what's good for society, but it's time now to emphasize that there's only one *actual* reality. And as Christians who believe the Bible is the inspired and authoritative Word of God, our answers to worldview questions must come from Scripture (going forward,

I'll refer to a worldview based on what the Bible teaches as the *biblical worldview*).[2] When Christians advocate for the common good, we need to do so with clarity on what the Bible teaches about the true nature of reality.

How Biblical Theology Informs the Good

We obviously can't do a comprehensive survey of everything the Bible teaches about reality here, but we're going to look at a selection of key theological points that have bearing on the subject of the common good in particular. We'll frame them around just two pivotal questions: Who is God? And who is man?

Who Is God?

It's easy to forget that when people invoke the name of God, they may be conceiving of Him in ways quite different from what the Bible teaches. As just one example, according to a 2022 Gallup survey, 81 percent of Americans say they believe in God, but only half of that group even believes God hears and answers prayers.[3] People today have many unbiblical conceptions about God, and those competing conceptions are often at the source of cultural debates over the common good. In the course of these cultural dialogues, Christians are often getting confused in their own understanding of who God is, so it's important to get back to basics. To that end, we're going to look at four biblical truths about who God is that are especially pertinent to the subject of this book: 1) God has revealed Himself through Scripture; 2) God has revealed Himself through the natural world; 3) God is love and defines love; and 4) God is just and defines justice.

1. God has revealed Himself Through Scripture.

This is one of the most fundamental truths of Christianity. Our God is not a deistic God who created the world and walked away, leaving us to blindly guess who He is, who we are, why we're here, and so on. God has revealed these things and much more in the Bible. That doesn't mean God revealed *everything* or even everything we'd like to know. But it does mean that we have the responsibility of knowing what He's told us and accepting those things as the truth about reality.

Recall that when it comes to defining the common good, this fact couldn't have greater significance. Unlike in a hypothetical universe without a God or in a universe created by a God who never revealed Himself, we have the ability to know that 1) objective truths pertaining to issues of cultural relevance exist, and 2) what those truths are. Yes, people in our culture may hold different worldviews, but that doesn't change what kind of universe we actually live in. There's only one reality, and it turns out it's the one in which the common good—what is morally right for and beneficial to communities of humans—is defined by and revealed by God. People may advocate for the common good according to their own definitions, but when those definitions don't line up with what God has revealed, we have to recognize that their ideas are objectively wrong and unashamedly advocate for the common good according to what is true.

Before we move on, it's worth noting that there are people who identify as Christians and yet don't believe the Bible is God's Word. Progressive Christians are those who typically view the Bible as man's evolving (and often errant) ideas about God rather than God's eternal truths revealed to man. Because progressive Christians don't recognize Scripture as authoritative revelation about reality, they'll naturally define the common good on their own subjective terms—just as someone who doesn't identify as a Christian at all would. And those terms typically line up with what is culturally acceptable. In fact, progressive Christians often condemn their Bible-believing counterparts for their views on social issues in the same way the culture at large does.[4] Thus, progressive Christians are usually not the object of cultural hate in the way that Christians who hold to the historic Christian faith are. When your authority for reality is yourself rather than the Bible, culture will warmly embrace you as one of its own—even if you technically call yourself a Christian.

2. God has revealed Himself through the natural world.

The Bible teaches that even if you never lay your hands on Scripture, there are certain things all people can and do know about God from the natural world (this is what theologians call *general revelation*). In Romans 1:18-20, the apostle Paul says,

> The wrath of God is revealed from heaven against all ungodliness and unrighteousness of men, who by their unrighteousness suppress the truth. For what can be known about God is plain to them, because God has shown it to them. For his invisible attributes, namely, his eternal power and divine nature, have been clearly perceived, ever since the creation of the world, in the things that have been made. So they are without excuse.

Don't miss the significance of this passage. Paul is saying that everyone clearly knows there's a divine and eternal Creator of the world just from observing creation, and if you deny that, you're suppressing the truth in unrighteousness; it's a *moral* problem. Furthermore, Paul says in Romans 2:14-16 that God gives humans innate knowledge of right and wrong (a moral conscience):

> When Gentiles, who do not have the law, by nature do what the law requires, they are a law to themselves, even though they do not have the law. They show that the work of the law is written on their hearts, while their conscience also bears witness, and their conflicting thoughts accuse or even excuse them on that day when, according to my gospel, God judges the secrets of men by Christ Jesus.

The fact that the Bible tells us all people have knowledge of a divine, eternal Creator and that He's given them a moral conscience—basic knowledge of right and wrong according to God's standards—has far-reaching implications for how we advocate for righteousness in the public square. In the words of philosophy professor J. Budziszewski, "One cannot convince people of what they already grasp; one can only draw it out of them…The one thing needful is to distinguish between those who are honestly confused and those who would only like to think they are."[5] When we learn how to engage graciously with and ask probing questions of culture on subjects like those we'll cover in part 2, always remember we're working to draw out what the Bible says they already know about the basic nature of reality.

3. God is love and defines love.

Culture largely assumes that both the importance and definition of love are self-evident. Phrases like *love is love* and *love is all you need* are plastered on T-shirts, billboards, and bumper stickers to persuade us all of how simple love should be to understand. And when we're talking about rescuing a kitten from a tree or heroically saving a child from drowning, people generally do agree on what a loving action is. But the shallow simplicity of bumper-sticker slogans is revealed when we begin asking other kinds of questions:

- Is it loving to take your children to a pride parade in order to teach them about "diversity"?

- Is it loving to make sure a pregnant teenager can get an abortion?

- Is it loving to encourage a five-year-old boy struggling with gender dysphoria to start living as a girl?

For many people in our culture, the answer to these questions is as simple and self-evident as the answer to the question of whether to rescue a drowning child: "Yes, these actions are loving. And if you can't understand that, there's something wrong with you." But just as we saw that the definition of good depends on the nature of the universe in which we live, so does the definition of love. *The Bible teaches that God is love (1 John 4:8), so His perfect character is the only valid standard for defining love.* If we instead use our own standards to define love, we will err. There will be actions we feel are loving that are actually worthy of condemnation and actions we feel are unloving that are actually worthy of praise.

In the Bible, one of the most important passages about love is Matthew 22:36-39. A Pharisee asked Jesus, "Teacher, which is the greatest commandment of the law?" Jesus replied:

> You shall love the Lord your God with all your heart and with all your soul and with all your mind. This is the great and first commandment. And a second is like it: You shall love your neighbor as yourself.

Note the hierarchy here. If Jesus says one commandment is the *greatest*, that implies any other commandments should be obeyed within that context. This tells us that what it means to love others depends on what it means to first love God. Thus, when we advocate for the common good out of our love for others, that advocacy must first be rooted in our love for and obedience to God.

4. God is just and defines justice.

Just as our culture loves love, our culture loves justice. In fact, the quest for social justice is one of the defining features of this cultural moment (more on that in chapter 7). But yet again, as Christians, we have to establish definitions according to the Bible.

There are multiple senses of the word *justice*, but the one most pertinent to the subject of this book is *making right that which is wrong*. As we've already discussed, right and wrong are moral categories that require a standard, and it's God's character that provides that standard. Deuteronomy 32:4 says, for example, "The Rock, his work is perfect, for all his ways are justice. A God of faithfulness and without iniquity, just and upright is he." Psalm 9:7-8 says, "The LORD sits enthroned forever; he has established his throne for justice, and he judges the world with righteousness; he judges the peoples with uprightness." Only God is perfectly righteous, and His perfectly righteous character is the objective standard by which He judges the world.

Importantly, God's people are also to judge, and we are to do so according to the standards He's revealed. If we instead use our own standards to define right and wrong, we'll incorrectly identify what wrongs need to be made right. *That means people can genuinely believe they're working for justice while perpetuating great injustices.* Reproductive justice, for example, is a euphemism for the so-called right to abortion—an action that commits a great injustice against a preborn baby. Our culture may love justice, but its concept of justice often has a problematic relationship with the reality of God's objective standards.

Who Is Man?

While the nature of mankind may sound like a lofty philosophical question devoid of practical significance, that couldn't be further from the truth. Divergent views on who or what a human being is are actually at the root of nearly every cultural debate today. Rev. Robert Sirico, cofounder of the Acton Institute, has put the pivotal nature of the question this way:

> If we don't get an understanding of who the human person
> is correct, anything else we build on that foundation will
> be faulty...And if there's any one great dilemma that we

can point to in our culture and our society today, it's that people don't know who they are.[6]

Culture may be confused about the nature of mankind, but Christians shouldn't be. Our Creator told us all we need to know about who we are. In particular, there are three biblical teachings regarding our identity that are foundational for thinking rightly about the common good: 1) every human is made in the image of God; 2) every human has an objective purpose; and 3) every human has a sin nature. Let's look at each one briefly.

1. Every human is made in the image of God.

Far from being accidental by-products of blind evolutionary processes, mankind was created by God in His own image (Genesis 1:26-27). The image of God refers to the immaterial aspects of our being—those that set us apart from animals. Unlike animals, we are moral creatures who are able to reflect, reason, and make the choices necessary to execute the dominion that God gave us over the earth (Genesis 1:28).

Because every human is created by and made in the image of God, every human is inherently and equally valuable. That means human value never depends on our abilities, size, accomplishments, or anything else. We have value because—and only because—God gives us that value. Our inherent value is what makes murder (the unjustified taking of innocent life) such an affront to God. Life is His to give and His to take.

2. Every human has an objective purpose.

As we just saw, humans have inherent and equal value because our Creator gave us that value. But God didn't give us value for the sake of giving us value. He created us *for* something—He gave us a purpose. The collective witness of Scripture is that we exist to know

God, love God, and make Him known to others (for example, see Hosea 6:6; Matthew 28:19; Luke 10:27; John 17:3; 1 Timothy 2:4). This is true for all people; human purpose is not a subjective, individualized adventure.

Recall from earlier why this fact is so important: We need to know the purpose of something to determine whether an action will be beneficial or harmful to it (recall the example of a hammer hitting a nail versus a hammer hitting a toy). In the same way, knowing what humans are "for" must inform the Christian understanding of how to advocate for the good of individuals and society. We'll see examples of this in chapters 9 and 10.

3. Every human has a sin nature.

According to the American Worldview Inventory conducted by Arizona Christian University's Cultural Research Center, 69 percent of Americans believe people are "basically good"—as do more than half of Christians whom researchers otherwise classified as having a biblical worldview.[7] Dr. George Barna, director of the research, subsequently identified this belief as one of the "Top 10 Most Seductive Unbiblical Ideas Americans Adopt." Why is it unbiblical? The Bible is clear from start to finish that humans have a sin nature. We are *not* basically good...we just like to think we are.

God created humans with the ability to choose between right and wrong, and when Adam and Eve disobeyed God, sin entered the world (Genesis 3). The consequence of sin is death (Romans 6:23). And "just as sin came into the world through one man, and death through sin, and so death spread to all men because all sinned" (Romans 5:12). Scripture leaves no doubt about this universal reach of our sin nature. Isaiah 53:6, for example, states, "All we like sheep have gone astray; we have turned—every one—to his own way." Ecclesiastes 7:20 says, "Surely there is not a righteous man on earth who does good and never sins." Romans 3:23 tells us, "All have sinned and fall short of the glory of God." And 1 John 1:8 says, "If we say we have no sin, we deceive ourselves, and the truth is not in us." As a culture, we've collectively deceived ourselves into thinking we're basically good, but the Bible tells a very different story.

What's Truly Good Is Often Hated

If you're somewhat new to theology or comparing worldviews and their implications, I realize this chapter may pose a bit of a learning curve. Go back and read it again if needed! Many people—both Christians and nonbelievers—have never considered all the worldview factors involved in determining what is good and what that means for the common good. As I said at the beginning of this chapter, these words sound self-explanatory. But it's the deceptive ease with which culture throws them around that often leads to the confusion we see today, both in and out of the church. We can't afford to not take the time to understand what's *truly* good—as defined by God—when so many lives are at stake. Ironically, what's truly good is often hated by culture, which makes it all the more pressing that Christians have clarity. Without clarity, we're prone to compromise truth under cultural accusations of hate.

Because this chapter is more conceptual in nature, you may already be wondering about some of the *how* questions. Don't worry—we'll get into a lot of specifics in part 2 on individual issues and what it looks like for Christians to advocate for the common good when it comes to some of the most controversial (non-soup kitchen) subjects today. But there are some additional important concepts we need to explore before we get there. In particular, we need clarity on the intersection of faith and politics…because sometimes advocating for the common good is political.

Yes, I said it. The forbidden *p* word.

It's a word with so much baggage in the church that it warrants not just one but two of its own chapters. To that end, let's go to chapter 3.

CHAPTER 2 SUMMARY

- The vast majority of culture wars today are over the common good. By and large, those wars aren't happening because some people want what's good for society and others don't. They're happening because people disagree on *what* is good for society.

- *Good* is defined as that which is 1) morally right or 2) beneficial to someone or something. Both of these meanings are inherently connected to a person's worldview.

- People may have all kinds of worldviews, leading to culture wars over what is best for society, but there's only one reality. When Christians advocate for the common good, we need to do so with clarity on what the Bible teaches.

- There are four biblical truths about who God is that are especially pertinent to the subject of this book: 1) God has revealed Himself through Scripture; 2) God has revealed Himself through the natural world; 3) God is love and defines love; and 4) God is just and defines justice.

- Likewise, there are three biblical truths regarding the identity of mankind that are foundational for thinking rightly about the common good: 1) every human is made in the image of God; 2) every human has an objective purpose; and 3) every human has a sin nature.

CHAPTER 3

WHEN THE COMMON GOOD IS POLITICAL

*Advocating for the common good out of our love
for others sometimes includes the political.*

■ ■ ■

Should Christians be political?

Of course we should.

That answer shouldn't be controversial, yet I am well aware that some readers just got a bit nervous. *This is going to get unnecessarily divisive. Does she really have to talk about politics?*

Other readers care deeply about politics and just got appreciably more excited than they were while reading about the philosophical and theological context of the term *common good* in chapter 2. *Okay, now she's getting practical. Let's talk about the crazy direction of this country and what we can do about it.*

Still others are deeply ambivalent. Frankly, that was me for most of my life. My husband cared significantly more about politics than I did for many years of our marriage, and I would often express my bewilderment at his interest with sentiments like the following: "I just don't get why people care about this bill or that bill or what this candidate is doing and why that candidate failed. It's so…boring. And I'm just one person with absolutely no say other than a single vote in an occasional election." If you can relate, you're probably think-ing, *I just hope the rest of this book isn't about politics. I can only han-dle one chapter.* I get it.

I'm guessing most readers lean more or less toward one of these three postures: politically hesitant, politically passionate, or politically ambivalent. My not-so-small goal in this chapter is to cast a vision for Christian engagement with politics that's compelling to readers of any starting posture. If Christians are indeed called to advocate for righteousness on behalf of the common good (as we've seen is the case in the prior two chapters), we need to recognize that our calling will inevitably often overlap with the political process in some way. As such, we need a healthy view of what it can and should mean for Christians to be political.

Clearing the Baggage

Before readers of varied political postures can move forward together on this subject, we need to find some common ground from which to begin. But I believe there are two persistent factors that typically prevent Christians from finding that necessary starting point.

First, we're often working from some very different presuppo-sitions about what the words *politics* and *political* mean. Given the often-heated nature of the subject, everyone is carrying some kind of baggage into the conversation, but we rarely stop to identify what those preconceived notions are. For example, when one person thinks of the intersection between politics and faith, they're immediately repulsed because they're thinking of biblically inappropriate con-flations of love for country and love for God. Another person is thinking of all the painful tensions they've experienced while having conversations on controversial topics with both Christians and non-believers. Someone else is thinking of pastors they believe are prior-itizing political activism over the discipleship of their congregation. And yet another person isn't thinking of anything beyond the idea that Christians can and should vote when an election arises. Those are just a few examples, but if you asked each of these hypothetical people whether Christians should be political without stopping to define what you mean, you would get some very different answers rooted in some very different assumptions.

So, let's put some bags down.

At the most basic level, politics is "the way that people living in groups make decisions."[1] In other words, politics is the process through which people living in communities decide on the parameters of how they're going to live together—what their life in *common* will look like. In modern contexts, this typically relates to the activities of what we more formally call *government*—the entity invested with the authority to make and enforce laws for a defined community (often a state or nation). When I started this chapter by asking whether Christians should be involved in politics and answered in the affirmative, this is the relatively bag-free sense I had in mind. *Christians who live in countries with the opportunity to influence the governing structure toward making and enforcing laws that promote the common good should embrace that opportunity out of a love for others.* This should be a pretty uncontroversial statement as expressed, but nonetheless, we'll talk about the biblical warrant for it shortly. For now, I simply want to establish a basic working definition of the political, stripped away from the layers of baggage that often accompany it.

A second factor that prevents Christians from finding common starting ground on politics is that we get stuck in a mire of warnings about how one might err in applying faith to politics without ever developing a *positive* view of engagement beyond that. Consider the following illustration to see why this is so problematic.

Imagine that a child asks her parent how to best ride a bike. The parent responds, "Bike riding is dangerous because there are drivers who won't see you." When the child asks again about how to ride, the parent responds, "You can ride too fast and fall off." Again, the child asks and the parent replies, "You can put your foot in the pedal incorrectly and get stuck." After a while, the child concludes that bike riding is a problematic activity in and of itself because all she ever heard was warnings about what can go wrong; *errors* in bike riding became synonymous with the *activity* of bike riding.

In the same way, there's been a proliferation of content today focused on warnings about potential errors in Christian political engagement—books, articles, podcasts, and even church curricula. Some of the most frequently raised concerns include the following (for the record, I'll add a very brief response to each one):

- *Christians shouldn't conflate love for country with love for God.* Agreed. The greatest commandment is to love God with all our heart, soul, and mind (Matthew 22:37). Loving anything more than or the same as God is idolatry, and that includes one's country.

- *Christians shouldn't place political tribalism over truth.* Agreed. *Nothing* should be placed over truth (political or otherwise). We are Christians in our identity before anything else.

- *Christians shouldn't look to politics as their savior.* Agreed. Government is a temporal institution incapable of creating an earthly utopia because evil will continue to exist until the end of time. No matter how well a government functions, it won't save you from earthly strife, nor will it save your soul.

- *Christians shouldn't engage in political discussions in uncharitable, ungracious ways.* Agreed. Christians are just as guilty as anyone of being jerks. We should strive for graciousness in discussions of all kinds.

These are all worthwhile concerns to raise and warnings to heed. In fact, biblically speaking, no Christian should disagree with *any* of these four points. But like the parent who only ever talks about ways to err in bike riding and never moves on to talk about how to ride well, this cottage industry of "warning" content rarely gets past its critique of Christian errors to cast a positive vision of how Christians *should* engage politically. And if anything at all is addressed to that end, it's often implied that the solution is to effectively disengage and treat all political positions as equally plausible for Christians of good conscience...lest we fall into one of these errors.

If I may be blunt, this is intellectual and spiritual laziness.

Possible errors in political engagement are not the same as political engagement itself being inherently problematic. Yes, we need to acknowledge possible pitfalls, but we must then be willing to do the hard work of seeking a positive vision beyond them and deriving our positions from biblical truth.

With the objective of clearing baggage and finding common ground, we can add to our earlier starting point, then, as follows:

Christians who live in countries with the opportunity to influence the governing structure toward making and enforcing laws that promote the common good should embrace that opportunity out of a love for others. In doing so, we shouldn't conflate love for country with love for God, place political tribalism (or anything at all) over truth, look to politics as our savior, or engage in ungracious, uncharitable ways.

This, of course, still leaves plenty of room for disagreement among Christians in the particulars of application, but that's okay. We had to put some bags down to have fresh eyes for the discussion ahead. Now we're in a position to get more specific. Let's start by looking at what the Bible tells us about God's purpose for government.

God's Purpose for Government

The Bible says relatively little specific to how Christians should relate to and engage in influencing the governing structure under which they live. This has led some people to conclude that it's forbidden, undesirable, or at the very least unimportant for Christians to be involved in the political sphere. However, these conclusions don't follow either from what the Bible *does* teach about government or from an understanding of Jesus's historical-political context.

Consider first some key points on what the Bible teaches about government.

In the Old Testament, the first mention of what could be considered civil government is in Genesis 9:5-6, when Noah and his family exit the ark after the flood. God says He will require a reckoning for murder to be carried out *by human beings*: "Whoever sheds the blood of man, by man shall his blood be shed, for God made man in his own image." While there are no further details, the basic principle that mankind is responsible for executing punishment for certain actions is assumed throughout the rest of the Bible. For example, in the Old Testament, when God calls out nations for not practicing righteousness and justice, that assumes an expectation that civil leaders are responsible for promoting what is good and restraining what is evil (see Proverbs 31:8-9; Daniel 4:27; Amos 1–2; Obadiah). In the New Testament, this expectation is most explicitly stated in Romans 13:1-7. Because this passage is particularly important, we'll read it in its entirety:

> Let every person be subject to the governing authorities. For there is no authority except from God, and those that exist have been instituted by God. Therefore whoever resists the authorities resists what God has appointed, and those who resist will incur judgment. For rulers are not a terror to good conduct, but to bad. Would you have no fear of the one who is in authority? Then do what is good, and you will receive his approval, for he is God's servant for your good. But if you do wrong, be afraid, for he does not bear the sword in vain. For he is the servant

of God, an avenger who carries out God's wrath on the wrongdoer. Therefore one must be in subjection, not only to avoid God's wrath but also for the sake of conscience. For because of this you also pay taxes, for the authorities are ministers of God, attending to this very thing. Pay to all what is owed to them: taxes to whom taxes are owed, revenue to whom revenue is owed, respect to whom respect is owed, honor to whom honor is owed.

From this passage, we can derive three pivotal biblical teachings on government that should shape our views today.

First, civil rulers receive their authority from God Himself, and as such are His servants (vv. 1-4). This means that the institution of civil government is a good thing! Christians can sometimes be so critical of government that they forget (or perhaps never knew) this is a clear biblical teaching. That doesn't mean, however, that everything civil government does is good or that Christians should be in limitless obedience to government. As we've already seen, the Bible has many examples of rulers doing evil in spite of their God-given role. The role is good, but the execution of the role by sinful humans won't always be. Because of this reality of living in a fallen world, most Christians throughout history have believed that there are times when civil disobedience is appropriate—in particular, when there's a conflict between obedience to God and obedience to government. And Scripture provides us with several precedents for this kind of disobedience. For example, in Acts 4:18, the apostles are commanded to stop preaching the gospel. But they made their position clear to the high priest: "We must obey God rather than men" (Acts 5:29). In other words, their highest authority was God, who called them to preach the gospel (Matthew 28:16-20), so when other (lower) authorities contradicted that command, their allegiance was first to God. Some other examples include the Hebrew midwives in Exodus 1; Rahab in Joshua 2; Shadrach, Meshach, and Abednego in Daniel 3; Daniel in Daniel 6; and the wise men in Matthew 2.

Second, civil rulers should be God's servants for promoting the good (v. 4). Whereas Genesis 9:5-6 explicitly affirms only civil *punishment*, Romans 13:1-7 also explicitly affirms the civil role of promoting the good (which, as we saw, is already implied in the rest of Scripture by references to the necessity of advocating for righteousness). Specifics aren't given on the various forms of the good that God's servants should promote, so even among Christians who agree this is a role of government, there will always be some disagreements. In modern society, for example, should government provide the good of healthcare for all? How about the good of public education? Or the goods of national security, infrastructure, or national parks? In at least some sense, all of these examples *could* be defined as a good. Yet we all recognize that there's a limit to what government can provide because financial resources are finite; we can't have every good we might theoretically want. So while it's a biblical principle that civil governments should indeed promote the good, Christians will still inevitably disagree on how to prioritize individual goods their government might pursue.

Third, civil rulers have the authority to bear the sword as avengers on God's behalf (v. 4). Here again we see that God has given humans—through civil government—the authority to punish evil. God will, of course, vanquish all evil at the end of time, but civil government has the role of restraining evil now. Christians sometimes object to this idea by pointing out that Jesus said, "If anyone slaps you on the right cheek, turn to him the other also" (Matthew 5:39). But in the context of the Sermon on the Mount, Jesus is talking about personal conduct, not the role of governing institutions. In other words, if someone insults you (slaps you on the cheek), let them. But when justice is necessary, civil rulers are God's agents for carrying it out.

These three principles from Romans 13 provide a foundational framework within which we as Christians should consider our political engagement (it's worth noting that these same principles are repeated and encapsulated in 1 Peter 2:13-14: "Be subject for the Lord's sake to every human institution, whether it be to the emperor as supreme, or to governors as sent by him to punish those who do evil and to praise those who do good"). *The Bible is clear that civil government plays a vital and God-given role in our earthly communities.* Because civil leaders are to be in service to God, the good they promote and the evil they restrain should be aligned with godly definitions of those terms (see chapter 2). When we live in a historical-political context in which we have the opportunity to influence our government to promote what is (truly) good and restrain what is (truly) evil, we should embrace that opportunity, knowing that we are advocating for government to function as God intended.

That brings me to our second point in response to the idea that it's forbidden, undesirable, or unimportant for Christians to be involved in political influence just because the Bible says relatively little specific to such action: This conclusion ignores Jesus's historical-political context.

When Jesus was born, the land of Israel had been under the control of the Roman Empire for about 60 years. The area had traded hands between major empires—Assyria, Babylon, Persia, and Greece—for hundreds of years before that.[2] In spite of the perennial Jewish desire for political independence, the possibility seemed distant to most by the time Jesus was born. The area was a relatively remote outpost under the domination of a vast empire centered hundreds of miles away.

This tidbit of history is quite important for understanding why Jesus wouldn't have talked more specifically about the need for His disciples to influence government. *They had very little opportunity to do so at the time.* Jesus first and foremost came as the long-awaited Messiah, who would give His life as a ransom for many (Mark 10:45) and rise from the dead to give the hope of eternal life to those who place their trust in Him for forgiveness of sins. Teaching and demonstrating that the kingdom of God had come near was necessarily the focus of His three years of public ministry (Luke 10:9). Because of this priority and the brevity of His mission, Jesus didn't directly address all kinds of subjects we normally consider important for Christians to care about given what we know from the full witness of Scripture—for example, child abuse, infanticide, racism, or domestic violence.

Jesus's silence on a given subject, therefore, doesn't imply that subject is forbidden, undesirable, or unimportant for Christians to care about. We have to consider the entirety of Scripture, because *all* Scripture "is breathed out by God and profitable for teaching" (2 Timothy 3:16). Given that there was little near-term opportunity for a new religious movement to directly advocate for sweeping changes to the policies of a vast empire, it makes sense that Jesus didn't explicitly speak to that need. At the same time, we've seen that the Bible, in its entirety, provides many relevant principles that indicate the vital role Christians should play in advocating for righteousness in the public square: passages like Romans 13:1-7 and 1 Peter 2:13-14; Old Testament references to the importance of justly functioning societies; the ways in which biblical figures engaged with civil authorities; and the broader implications of Jesus's exhortation to be salt and light.

We should never develop our views from less than what the Bible teaches, so our biblical exploration thus far has been a necessary starting point. However, none of this has been said to suggest that there's enough stated in the Bible to create anything resembling a complete theology of political engagement. As with many subjects, we have to develop our specific views as an inference from broader biblical principles.

It's outside the scope of this book to provide a detailed discussion on how Christians have developed varied political views throughout church history, but it's worthwhile to close with a brief overview of some major historical developments that provide helpful context for us today.[3]

Politics in Light of Church History

In the first three centuries after Jesus lived on Earth, both Jews and Christians were oppressed by the Roman Empire for refusing to acknowledge the divinity of the emperor. The intensity and geographic focus of persecution varied over time, but broadly speaking, Christianity was illegal, and Christians had to practice their faith in secret. Because of these circumstances, developing a detailed political theology of how best to influence government for the common good or for the restraint of evil wasn't a priority; there was very little they could do. Their primary witness to government at the time was focused on obeying the law, paying taxes, and fulfilling the basic duties of being good Roman subjects.

Everything changed radically when Christianity was not only legalized in AD 313, but was also made the *official religion* of the Roman Empire in AD 380. As you might imagine, this suddenly raised all kinds of questions for Christians that had previously been moot. Now the church had the power to have almost unlimited influence in governing a wide swath of society. What, exactly, should that look like? This newly relevant and urgent question was the subject of much consideration by Christian theologians over the next millennium, from Augustine of Hippo's classic political work *The City of God* in AD 426 to the expositions of prominent medieval thinkers like Thomas Aquinas and William of Ockham on natural law.

The next radical societal shift started when Martin Luther challenged the practices and teachings of the Catholic Church in 1517, kicking off what came to be known as the Protestant Reformation. For hundreds of years prior, civil and religious (Catholic) authority had been intertwined and functioned closely together. But with the emergence of Protestantism, authorities now had to contend with a major religious split between the people under their rule—not to mention their own shifting religious convictions in some cases. Over time, this led to important new questions about the hierarchy of authority between church and state, as well as the relationship between individual Christians and the state.

One example of a major question raised in this post-Reformation world (and one that's still often at the forefront of discussions today) was the degree to which Christians should expect to influence their societies now that the church and state were no longer interconnected in the same way. Some were relatively skeptical about how much good could be accomplished in a fallen world. Luther himself is usually placed in this camp, following the earlier thinking of Augustine. Other post-Reformation thinkers were far more optimistic about the possibilities of Christian influence. There are all kinds of reasons why Christians have differed on their expectations in this area, but one reason often prominent today is that people have varied views on eschatology (end-times theology). Those who anticipate that the world will continually deteriorate until Jesus returns have tended to be less optimistic about the degree to which Christians can change society. Those who anticipate that the world will continually improve have tended to be more optimistic. But despite these differing expectations, nearly every Christian theological tradition has recognized that God established civil governments for the purpose of promoting good and restraining evil (per Romans 13) and that Christians have a role in advocating for righteousness in society accordingly.

The sociopolitical changes that took place in Europe as a result of the Reformation eventually gave rise to the development of liberal democracies with yet another new set of political questions. It was one thing for Protestants and Catholics to figure out how to live side by side in the years immediately after the Reformation; it's another thing for atheists, agnostics, Muslims, Jews, Christians, Mormons, and Buddhists to figure out how to best live together today (to name just a few worldview examples). Greg Forster, in his book *The Contested Public Square*, sums up the present challenge well:

> Premodern society had a shared religion and thus a shared conception of how the universe works…This shared worldview produced rules of social behavior, and the state was the enforcement mechanism by which society held its members to those rules. Modern society, by contrast, does not have a shared religion, and thus its members often disagree on things like metaphysics and ethics. The state is still an enforcement mechanism by which society holds its members to a set of rules, but those rules no longer grow from a shared worldview.[4]

In America, this reality is glaringly obvious today in a way it hasn't always been. Christianity was never the official religion of our country, but there's no question that it was the predominant worldview influence behind our founding and the worldview at least loosely held by most of its people over the last 400 years.[5] To be sure, we can't say with any historical accuracy that we were always bound together by a steadfast commitment to the core doctrines of Christianity. However, we can certainly say that for most of our history we were bound together by values *rooted* in the Christian worldview.

All that is changing now—and quickly.

As I explain in *Faithfully Different*:

> Though people have increasingly discarded the doctrinal specifics of Christianity over time, the societal result hasn't always been as obvious as it is today because people generally continued to hold values *consistent* with Christianity (for

example, the importance of the family unit, the nature of marriage, and the value of human life). But in more recent years, secular society has started discarding the long hangover of Christian *values* as well. Christianity no longer looks like a contemporary cousin to the mainstream worldview. Today it's more like a distant ancestor who no longer shares recognizable traits.[6]

This statement is not based on mere perception. Research shows that these changes have been happening rapidly in recent years. According to the Pew Research Center, as of 2019, about 65 percent of Americans self-identify as Christians. That number was 77 percent only 12 years prior, and a drop has occurred in almost every Christian denomination. Of course, those numbers only tell you how people identify themselves—not what they actually believe. Research on people's beliefs is far more grim. According to the American Worldview Inventory I referenced in chapter 2, only about *4 percent* of Americans hold beliefs consistent with the core truths of what the Bible teaches, and that number has been dropping precipitously over the last 25 years.[7]

Furthermore, those who no longer identify as Christians are overwhelmingly now identifying as atheists, agnostics, or "nothing in particular" (collectively called the "nones")—worldviews at fundamental odds with Christianity. The percentage of Americans holding these worldviews has grown from 17 to 26 percent in just the last decade, and the trend is seen across nearly every group: whites, blacks, Hispanics, men, women, geographic areas, and educational attainment. It's even more prominent among millennials; a full 40 percent of them now identify as a "none."

Yes, America is changing fast.

We're standing at a crossroads, and we must take that seriously. While Christians sometimes consider politics to be an unnecessary distraction to the church, history begs to differ. As we've seen, political questions aren't the myopic domain of twenty-first century Western Christians who want to entertain a hobby interest in how their societies function. These questions have been of pressing importance and necessity for more than 1,700 years.

When the Common Good Is Political

Oftentimes, people today lament the political polarization we see as if it's just a function of no one *wanting* to get along. But our present-day polarization isn't a reflection of gratuitous disagreement over trivial matters. It's a reflection of the seismic split that has happened in people's underlying views on the nature of reality.

Lest anyone underestimate the implications, let's be clear: Non-Christian views of reality are not only wrong but are often destructive when taken to their natural conclusion in the political domain. Those who believe preborn babies are merely clumps of cells will want to enshrine a right to destroy those "cells" at will in law. Those who believe that the nuclear family is a socially constructed "obstacle to human freedom" will advocate for laws that weaken the institution of marriage and parental rights.[8] Those who believe that children are fundamentally sexual creatures will seek legal avenues for introducing sexually explicit content to public school kids at younger and younger ages. Those who believe that moral disagreement is hate will advocate for greater limits on freedom of speech and restrictions on religious liberty.

What an enormous and urgent opportunity we have to be light in this darkening culture.

To be sure, the light we need to shine today often has nothing to do with politics. In fact, in part 2, we'll see plenty of ideas for how to advocate for the common good in the nonpolitical realm; this isn't a book that's limited to questions of political engagement. But *when* the common good is of a political nature, as it often is, we must take seriously the opportunity we have to influence government in a godly way.

Not because we want to "war" with culture, but because we love God and because we love people.

CHAPTER 3 SUMMARY

- Politics is the process through which people living in communities decide on the parameters of how they're going to live together.

- Christians who live in countries with the opportunity to influence the governing structure toward making and enforcing laws that promote the common good should embrace that opportunity out of a love for others.

- Possible errors in political engagement are not the same as political engagement itself being inherently problematic.

- Three key biblical teachings on the nature of government are: 1) Civil rulers receive their authority from God Himself and as such are His servants; 2) civil rulers should be God's servants for promoting the good; and 3) civil rulers have the authority to bear the sword as avengers on God's behalf.

- In light of history, it makes sense that Jesus wouldn't have talked more specifically about the need for His disciples to influence government; they had very little opportunity to do so at the time.

- We must take seriously the occasion we have to influence government in a godly way—not because we want to "war" with culture, but because we love God and because we love people.

CHAPTER 4

SHOULD CHRISTIANS IMPOSE THEIR VIEWS ON OTHERS?

And four other objections to public Christian influence

■ ■ ■

In chapter 3, we looked at key biblical principles on the nature of government and some relevant historical context. Those points are an important foundation for thinking rightly about advocating for the common good in the political realm. That said, I would be naïve to move on without acknowledging some common objections.

There are still a few bags we need to put down.

I think it's fair to say that the typical Christian objections to political involvement today are not about the finer theological points of Romans 13. Nor are they usually in reference to the complex political theologies that have developed over the last several hundred years.[1] When those who lean toward politically hesitant or politically ambivalent positions object in some degree to Christian political involvement, it typically sounds more like this:

Christians shouldn't impose their views on others.

Christians shouldn't seek power.

Getting involved in politics harms our witness.

Political divisions disrupt unity in the church.

Christians shouldn't be partisan.

These and similar ideas have become like mantras within the church—phrases we hear so often that we've stopped thinking deeply about their validity. On the surface, they sound good. But, as we'll see in this chapter, they break down in light of biblical teaching, logic, or both. (Note that we'll evaluate challenges to Christian political involvement posed by those *outside* the church in chapter 6.)

Responding to the Objections
Objection 1: Christians shouldn't impose their views on others.

This objection is one that often comes from outside the church, but many Christians have come to believe it as well. After all, culture regularly tells us that one of the highest virtues is tolerance and that separation of church and state is central to our democracy. If you put these two culturally cherished ideas together, imposing anything on anyone sounds repugnant, and imposing religious ideas in the public domain sounds like a violation of our nation's founding principles. As a result, Christians sometimes end up making statements like the following: "I'm firmly pro-life, but I don't think I should impose my views on other people. Women have to decide what's best for them."

So let's look at this objection about imposing one's views on others more closely. To *impose* means to force something to be accepted by someone else. In the political context, we're talking about the legal force of policy decisions. Thus, the question becomes, Is it problematic for Christians to impose their views on others by advocating for the legal force of our desired policies?

Not at all.

In *every* matter of policy, *someone* is imposing their view on someone else.

If we pass laws against speeding, we're imposing the view that speeding is harmful on those who don't think it is. If we pass laws against theft, we're imposing the view that theft is wrong on those who would like to shoplift consequence-free. If we pass laws against pedophilia, we're imposing the view that pedophilia is wrong on those who believe it's a natural and harmless orientation that should be fulfilled. I could keep going, but you get the idea. It's not somehow unkind to or intolerant of others when you advocate for laws that reflect your viewpoint. *That's just the nature of public policy.* It's no more intolerant of you to advocate for a policy rooted in your view than it is for someone with an opposing position to advocate for a policy rooted in theirs.

But what about religious views more specifically? Doesn't the Constitution prohibit imposing religious views on others?

It depends on what you mean by imposing religious views.

The First Amendment of the US Constitution says, "Congress shall make no law respecting an establishment of religion, or prohibiting the free exercise thereof." This statement, known as the Establishment Clause, ensures that the government will not establish a state-supported church and will not force individuals to practice a specific religion; it cannot "impose" religious views in that way. This is what it means that the United States is a secular country—we're not committed to the authority of any particular religion in public life.[2] Note, however, that the Establishment Clause says nothing about how individuals should or should not use their religious beliefs to inform their participation in the political process. This is a key distinction.

Christians aren't in a special category of people who can't or shouldn't participate in the political process just because their views are religiously motivated; what motivates *any* person's political views is neither here nor there (if motivation were a consideration, we would be psychologically profiling people all day long!). Our country isn't committed to the authority of a particular religion, but individuals who *are* have every right to bring their views into the public square and vote accordingly.

Objection 2: Christians shouldn't seek power.

Let me ask you a hypothetical question: If someone offered you the power to end human trafficking, would you take it?

That's not a trick question. Assuming it wouldn't involve a morally problematic tradeoff and that you had the mental and physical capabilities to execute the power, of course you would.

While that should be obvious, the word *power* has come to have such negative connotations today that it's at the root of a frequent objection to Christian political involvement (again, from both outside and inside the church). When Christians seek political positions or political influence of any kind, they're often accused of being power-hungry or power-worshippers, as if everyone should realize that seeking power is inherently bad.

But power is just the authority and ability to execute a governing role. It can be used well or it can be used poorly. If power were inherently a problem, we would need to get rid of government entirely, because government, by definition, is the body to which we give the power to make, enforce, and judge the laws of this country. As long as we have a government, someone will be in power, and those in power obviously sought that power. Thus, it doesn't make sense to chastise any one group for being power-hungry simply for desiring the power necessary for public influence. As Christians, our desire should be to give power to those who will steward it well—to promote what's good and restrain what's evil (see chapter 3). We should be mindful that Christians (like anyone else) can seek power for the wrong reasons or use power in ungodly ways. But that's not a problem with power—that's a problem with the abuse of it.

Now, sometimes the objection from within the church takes on a theological nature. For example, an oft-repeated idea is that Jesus gave up *His* power on the cross, so we should give up power as well. But this is problematic reasoning in two ways. First, it's not even an accurate characterization of the cross. Jesus willingly laid down His life for mankind (John 10:18). While it may have looked to people like He was defeated by the cross, in reality, Jesus's atoning death and subsequent resurrection were the greatest victories of all time. As fully man and fully God, Jesus was and still is sovereign over all things.

But let's say for the sake of argument that Jesus did in some vague sense give up power by allowing Himself to be crucified for mankind. Does it follow from the nature of Jesus's atoning death that Christians should not influence their governments to make and enforce laws that promote the common good? That would be a very hard case to make. Just because Jesus didn't achieve *one* type of good (spiritual atonement) through political processes doesn't mean we shouldn't achieve *other* types of good through those processes. Of course, it would be possible that such activities are prohibited elsewhere in the Bible, but as we saw in chapter 3, that's not the case. It's the consistent witness of Scripture that God cares about the just and righteous functioning of societies—the godly application of *power* by the rulers God has sovereignly put in place. To suggest that Jesus gave up His power on the cross, and therefore we should give up ours as well, is to equivocate between spiritual and social senses of the term and ignore the rest of Scripture.

Objection 3: Getting involved in politics harms our witness.

People use the phrase *harms our witness* in a lot of different ways, but generally speaking, this objection is that culture won't like us if we're involved in the public square, and if they don't like us, they won't want to hear the gospel. Because the gospel is of primary importance, we should avoid political subjects (or so the thinking goes).

In one sense, there's truth here. The Public Religion Research Institute, for example, reports that of the Americans who left their childhood religion as adults, 16 percent said they did so because their church was too focused on politics (whatever "too" focused may have meant to survey respondents).[3] And if you pay any attention at all to the mainstream news, you'll know that culture indeed despises when Christians advocate for policies consistent with a biblical worldview and in opposition to the popular moral consensus (more on that and the frequently lobbed accusation of "Christian nationalism" in chapter 6).

But it's important to recognize that this is nearly always a unidirectional concern. Culture doesn't like it when Christians advocate for what are typically considered to be conservative causes (for example, the subjects we'll cover in part 2), but culture opens its arms wide to Christians who advocate for what are typically considered to be progressive causes. For example, in a *New York Times* article titled "Progressive Christians Arise! Hallelujah!," writer Nicholas Kristof makes the case that with an increasing number of progressive Christians in government, "faith becomes more complicated in America," to which he responds, "Thank God."[4] He laments the fact that Christians are monolithically associated with conservatism and celebrates the fact that there are now more and more politicians in government who identify as Christians and promote progressive causes. One cannot even fathom *The New York Times* printing an opinion piece titled "Conservative Christians Arise! Hallelujah!" and celebrating a growth in the percent of Christian politicians advocating for conservative causes. That's because the cultural dislike of Christians in politics nearly always goes in only one direction. If you agree with culture in your political positions, they'll like you just fine. So, it's not Christian involvement in politics they don't like, it's Christian involvement in *conservative* politics they don't like.

With this in mind, the question becomes, Should Christians not advocate for politically *unpopular* positions out of concern for the gospel? To answer that, we have to recognize that we're not talking about things like whether local zoning laws should allow for a new McDonald's to be built on a given street corner. Christians who share a conviction about the authority of God's Word and agree on who God is, who man is, and other key biblical doctrines can legitimately disagree on the placement of a restaurant. But, in this book, we're talking about issues on which we can draw clear positions from biblical teachings. Not only are these issues on which we can draw clear positions, they're also issues of immense significance for the common good—life-and-death issues for millions of people in some cases. *If these positions logically follow from a biblical worldview, are we not downplaying the significance of the gospel itself by refusing to speak to how the gospel transforms our entire view of reality?* The gospel isn't some otherworldly thing wherein we casually say we'll take Jesus up on His offer of forgiveness in the afterlife and then keep on living however and believing whatever we want here.

People will be offended by the gospel alone. They'll also be offended by the truths that underlie the gospel and the truths that flow from the implications of the gospel. We can't separate all that to somehow minimize the offense—it's all one package of things that are true. There will be some who want to hear that full witness and some who don't (Matthew 13:1-23). But hiding part of the truth about reality in the hope that people will like us enough to hear the rest is at best cowardly and at worst a silent complicity with some of the greatest evils being perpetrated by society today. Do what's right and leave the results to God.

Objection 4: Political divisions disrupt unity in the church.

In an increasingly polarized culture, many Christians have experienced what I call *disagreement fatigue*. We're so tired of the many cultural disagreements with both fellow Christians and nonbelievers that we long for peace through unity. And especially within the church, we know unity is essential for followers of Jesus. In John 17:20-23, Jesus Himself prayed the following:

> I do not ask for these only, but also for those who will believe in me through their word, that they may all be one, just as you, Father, are in me, and I in you, that they also may be in us, so that the world may believe that you have sent me. The glory that you have given me I have given to them, that they may be one even as we are one, I in them and you in me, that they may become perfectly one, so that the world may know that you sent me and loved them even as you loved me.

So, yes, we must acknowledge that unity is vital (see also 1 Corinthians 1:10; Philippians 2:1-2; Titus 3:9). Unfortunately, however, we're sometimes pursuing unity at all costs, including the cost of truth. But the Bible never suggests that we should sacrifice truth in order to achieve some kind of polite collective agreement in the vague name of unity. In fact, the Bible repeatedly teaches to *divide* from those who are not holding to truth. For example, in Romans 16:17, Paul says, "I appeal to you, brothers, to watch out for those who cause divisions and create obstacles contrary to the doctrine that you have been taught; avoid them." Similarly, Paul warns Titus of those who are stirring up "foolish controversies," among other things (Titus 3:9). He then tells him, "As for a person who stirs up division, after warning him once and then twice, have nothing more to do with him, knowing that such a person is warped and sinful; he is self-condemned" (vv. 10-11). And in Jude 1:18-19, Jude says, "They said to you, 'In the last time there will be scoffers, following their own ungodly passions.' It is these who cause divisions, worldly people, devoid of the Spirit."

In none of these cases do writers of the New Testament say, "We need unity, so please be one with these people holding ungodly, erroneous beliefs. Prevent division at all costs!" Instead, they consistently advise the church to divide from those in error so they can be unified around truth.

What we should take away from this is that some divisions are bad and *some are actually good*. Divisions due to the unresolved presence of error in the church are bad, while divisions resulting from the removal of that error are good. Our goal, then, shouldn't be to prevent division, but rather, to divide rightly.

Some may respond, "Well, that's just about doctrine, like the fact that Jesus rose from the dead. That doesn't apply to political issues!" Of course we don't want to divide from one another over trivial issues, and that includes politically trivial issues. But imagine someone in the early church saying, "I'm a Christian! I believe Jesus rose from the dead, and I've accepted His forgiveness of sin. But I believe we should be able to kill whomever we want." Or imagine that Drag Queen Story Hour existed in the first century and one of Paul's church plants wanted to host it. Do we really think the early church would not have considered these to be grave errors worthy of division?

Just as I said earlier about the gospel, there are many truths that underlie doctrine more broadly and truths that flow from the implications of it. We can't neatly delineate between doctrine and its applications just because an issue happens to currently be something of a heated "political" nature.

To be sure, there's a lot of territory between trivial issues (things we should never divide over) and a belief like people should be able to kill whomever they want (something clearly worth dividing over). In the middle, there are all kinds of political gray areas where Christians may disagree on the particulars of policy while agreeing on underlying doctrinal principles. For example, we should all agree that prospective immigrants are image bearers of God who deserve to be treated with dignity, but we may disagree over how many people should be legally allowed to enter the country each year. Policy disagreements such as this are typically *not* matters to divide churches over.

So, in response to the objection that political divisions disrupt unity in the church, we can certainly say that's sometimes true. There are plenty of times when our sinful pride can lead to divisions that should never have happened and *do* disrupt what should have been biblical unity around doctrinal essentials, their underlying truths, and the implications that flow from them. *But the fact that poorly justified divisions sometimes take place doesn't mean biblically justified divisions are to be avoided by sweeping politically controversial subjects under the pew.* Remember, division itself isn't the problem. Wrong division is. If there are clear biblical positions on political issues of great significance for the common good, we should rightly divide. Biblical unity revolves around truth, not polite agreement where no agreement should be found.

Objection 5: Christians shouldn't be partisan.

Recall the research I cited earlier that 16 percent of Americans who left their childhood religion as adults did so because their church was too focused on politics. In response to that statistic, megachurch pastor Andy Stanley wrote in his bestselling book *Not in It to Win It: Why Choosing Sides Sidelines the Church*:

> Hundreds of thousands of people are represented in that statistic. They didn't leave the church because they found Jesus less compelling. They left because the church didn't find Jesus compelling enough. They recognized that when a church or church leader publicly lines up behind a candidate or party, they have abandoned the mission of Jesus.[5]

Stanley and like-minded authors make the case that it's highly problematic when the church is partisan—consistently siding with and being associated with one political party. The reasons they give for partisanship being problematic are varied, but they're typically connected to claims that partisanship is a sign the church has given in to political idolatry of some kind—we've "abandoned the mission" of Jesus, as Stanley said.

To answer this objection, let's do a brief thought experiment. Imagine we lived in a time and place where the biggest issue dividing two political parties was who people were allowed to worship. One political party advocated for policies enforcing the worship of the god Zeus, and the other advocated for the right to worship freely. If Christians—who believe that there is only one true God and that it's a sin to worship anyone or anything else—were all known for being affiliated with the latter party, would that be problematic? Would it signal political idolatry? Would it mean we had sold out to earthly concerns and abandoned the mission of Jesus? Of course not. It would be the logical outworking of what the parties stood for and how that lined up with what Christians believe.

In the same way, if one party aligns more with a biblical world-view on some of the most significant issues today, it's not inherently problematic that there would be a consistent association of Christians and that party. *It's what you would expect.* In fact, there are clear associations of other religious adherents and certain political parties as well. Consider these statistics:

- Of American adults who identify as Historically Black Protestants, 80 percent are/lean Democrat.

- Of American adults who identify as Buddhist, 69 percent are/lean Democrat.

- Of American adults who identify as Jewish, 64 percent are/lean Democrat.

- Of American adults who identify as Muslim, 62 percent are/lean Democrat.

These are just a few examples. But researchers found that more than half of *every* religious group leans Democrat except two: evangelical Protestants (56 percent lean Republican) and Mormons (70 percent lean Republican).[6] The four religious groups listed above have an even stronger political leaning than evangelical Christians, but people don't regularly talk about how Historically Black Protestants, Buddhists, Jews, and Muslims need to be less "partisan."

I think we can all see there's an elephant in the room. A Republican elephant. People tend to express concerns of partisanship only when they think Christianity is associated with unpopular conservative positions. But as we already saw in objection 3 (that getting involved in politics harms our witness), we shouldn't choose positions based on what's popular in order for the world to like us. If clear biblical positions on major issues line up more with one party than another, why would it be a problem if we're more often affiliated with that party? Logically speaking, partisanship is a nonissue.

That said, it's worth noting that when people claim Christians shouldn't be partisan, they're often understanding the word *partisan* to mean all kinds of other things that we *shouldn't* support. So, when I say partisanship isn't inherently an issue, that's *not* to say any of the following:

- that we should have our identity placed in a political party before it's placed in Jesus;

- that any given party fully or even mostly reflects biblical positions;

- that we should automatically support everything put forth by a party just because it's the party we often vote for;

- that we think politicians associated with a given party are necessarily of better character;

- that we don't think the party we typically vote for has its own problems with blind spots or corruption;

- that you aren't saved if you vote for a different party; or

- that you are saved if you support the party Christians are typically associated with.

We can agree on all of the above while recognizing that it's entirely possible biblical positions will line up more with one party than another. If that's the case and we appear to the world as politically one-sided, so be it.

A Test Case: Slavery

One belief that has nearly universal agreement in Western cultures today is that slavery was a devastating and evil institution. Thanks to the efforts of abolitionists in nineteenth-century America, slavery was eradicated in 1865 through the Thirteenth Amendment. The process of passing an amendment was, of course, political in nature. Yet virtually no one who objects to modern-day Christian political influence would claim that Christians should not have sought to end slavery just because it required involvement in the political process. That makes the issue of slavery a great test case for the validity of popular objections to political involvement today (recall that we used it as a test case in chapter 1 as well).

Here's how to apply it. When you encounter an objection, restate it using the preface "Christians shouldn't have worked to end slavery because [insert objection]." Chances are, you'll disagree with the statement. Asking yourself *why* will help reveal the underlying problem.

Let's try it using the objections we've covered in this chapter.

1. Christians shouldn't have worked to end slavery because we shouldn't have imposed our views on others.

There were plenty of people at the time—both Christians and nonbelievers—who wanted to keep slavery legal, so as always in public policy, one group's view was being imposed on another. But consider why we have no problem with the imposition of the abolitionist view today: Slavery is evil, and we don't want to live in a society where an evil institution is legal. We recognize that even if there are people who disagree that slavery is evil, they're objectively wrong, and we're happy to impose the morally correct view on them. Just as we wouldn't say, "I'm *antislavery*, but I don't want to impose my views on other people," we shouldn't say things like, "I'm *pro-life*, but I don't want to impose my views on other people." The question is what the right moral position is, not whether you should impose the right moral position on others.

2. Christians shouldn't have worked to end slavery because that involved seeking the power to do so.

Slavery was able to exist and thrive because it was legal in several states. In order to abolish slavery, people with the power to do so had to act. Fortunately, enough people in power—through the House of Representatives and the Senate—were able to pass the Thirteenth Amendment. We don't question their use of government power to do so because we recognize nearly universally today that that was the morally and therefore politically correct position to take. And no one would say that because Jesus "gave up" His power by dying on the cross, we shouldn't have used power to save millions of people from slavery. Those two matters have nothing to do with one another—neither in the case of slavery nor in the case of moral issues today.

3. Christians shouldn't have worked to end slavery because getting involved with a political issue harmed our witness.

Slavery treated people as dehumanized property, so the Christian abolitionist witness to the world was to boldly proclaim the objectively evil nature of slavery given that all people are image bearers of God. In fact, we mourn today that there were Christians who *didn't* recognize that truth at the time. If proslavery Americans didn't want to hear more about the good news of Jesus's sacrifice for their sins because they didn't like that this same truth meant their slaves were as human as they were, that wasn't a reason to stay silent. Christians who worked to eradicate slavery realized their witness in society was the gospel *plus* the advocacy for truths that flowed *from* the gospel.

4. Christians shouldn't have worked to end slavery because it disrupted unity in the church.

There's no question, historically speaking, that the issue of slavery disrupted unity in the church. Major Christian denominations permanently split over it. But no one today would chastise the churches who continued to speak out against slavery for not being quieter so they could have been unified with those who supported its continuation. We recognize that the unity of antislavery and proslavery positions *should* have been disrupted because one of those positions was in serious error.

5. Christians shouldn't have worked to end slavery because Christians shouldn't have been partisan.

Once again, it's telling that no one makes this kind of argument today. We aren't concerned with whether the antislavery position resulted in Christians taking sides with one particular party or not, and we don't accuse the abolitionist Christians of political idolatry for their one-sided involvement. We evaluate the issue itself (the morality of holding image bearers as property), we see it through the lens of what the Bible teaches, and we look back without concern for having taken sides because we realize there was only one morally correct side to take.

Christian Political Engagement Facilitates the Common Good

While there are plenty of other objections to Christian political engagement than the ones we've covered in this chapter, they're often extensions of these. For example, someone might say, "You can't legislate morality!," but that's merely a twist on "Christians shouldn't impose their views on others" (someone's morality is always being legislated). Or someone might say, "Christians shouldn't fight to get their own way," which is really a variation on "Christians shouldn't seek power" (if "their own way" is really God's way, then Christians shouldn't hesitate to seek power if they steward it well). And many others simply fall into the category of warnings rather than true objections, which we discussed in chapter 3.

When you use the slavery test to evaluate objections like these to Christian political involvement, it's fairly easy to see why they quickly lose force. It should be no different with modern issues of great moral significance for the common good. As we saw in chapter 3, when we have the opportunity to advocate for righteousness and against evil, we have the responsibility of doing so out of our love for others—whether it's an issue considered political or not.

CHAPTER 4 SUMMARY

- **Objection 1: Christians shouldn't impose their views on others.** In *every* matter of public policy, *someone* is imposing their view on someone else. That's just the nature of the process.

- **Objection 2: Christians shouldn't seek power.** Power is the authority and ability to execute a governing role. It can be used well or it can be used poorly. Thus, power isn't the problem, the abuse of power is.

- **Objection 3: Getting involved in politics harms our witness.** We shouldn't avoid taking politically unpopular positions out of concern for the gospel. When there are clear biblical positions on political issues, we downplay the significance of the gospel itself when we refuse to speak to how it transforms our entire view of reality.

- **Objection 4: Political divisions disrupt unity in the church.** Division itself isn't a problem. Wrong division is. If there are clear biblical positions on political issues of great significance for the common good, we should rightly divide.

- **Objection 5: Christians shouldn't be partisan.** If clear biblical positions on major issues line up more with one party's platform than another's, it's a logical outcome that we would more often be affiliated with that party. Partisanship itself is not inherently problematic.

CHAPTER 5

PERSEVERING IN THE PUBLIC SQUARE

*Know your (biblical) **A**uthority, strengthen*
*Conviction, and maintain **T**enacity (ACT).*

■ ■ ■

Part 1 of this book is titled "Understanding the Hate." As we come to the final chapter in this section, it's a good time to briefly recap what we've learned toward that end.

We saw in chapter 1 that culture refers to the people and institutions who hold the values considered to be in vogue for a given society. Importantly, culture functions as a gatekeeper of the ideas society deems admissible to the public square at any given time. Some groups with contrarian values never attempt to get past that gate because they have no desire to influence public opinion on how society should function. Culture, by and large, is fine with those groups.

But Christians are different. Not only are we a group with values directly opposed to many of those most cherished by culture today, but we *also* believe it's our God-given responsibility to influence the public square for the common good based on those values. While Christians aren't resented for everything we believe and do (remember, soup kitchens are fine!), culture increasingly hates us as a group for trying to get in the gate and is now actively working to keep our influence out. We'll see some specific examples of that in part 2.

The easy response would be a silent retreat, but the easy response is not a biblical one.

Jesus said we are to be salt and light, and that requires the public activities necessary for preserving the world and exposing darkness. Additionally, caring about the way society functions is part of following Jesus's second greatest commandment, to "love your neighbor as yourself" (Matthew 22:36-40). It's out of our love for others that we should unashamedly advocate for the common good in both the political and nonpolitical realms—a common good defined by God alone. Culture will inevitably call evil good and good evil (Isaiah 5:20), but our pursuit of what is *truly* good is more important than ever in a world increasingly embracing darkness. Jesus warned the world would hate us for it, but because we love Him, we persevere in obedience to His commands (John 14:15).

That brings us to our current junction. Part 1 has provided foundational theological, cultural, and civic context for considering the Christian's role in public influence. In part 2, we're going to apply that understanding to five specific issues that are of especially great significance for the common good today. Before we get there, however, there's a connecting subject we need to discuss in this final chapter of part 1: What will it take to persevere on the forthcoming issues—and those we don't discuss in this book—knowing culture will hate you for your stand?

Perseverance in the face of hate isn't easy. It's one thing to know you *should* advocate for the common good on these issues, but it's another thing to actually do it. There's often a significant cost involved. If we don't carefully consider what's required for perseverance, we likely won't get involved at all—either out of ambivalence or fear.

In this chapter, we'll consider what's necessary for perseverance through the framework of a short acronym (ACT): Know your (biblical) authority; strengthen conviction; and maintain tenacity.

Know Your (Biblical) **A**uthority

Let me point out what's hopefully obvious: There will be a huge difference in your motivation to persevere through hardship for the common good if you're confident the God of the universe has told you to do so.

If a given issue is something you kinda sorta think is something God kinda sorta cares about, do you really think you'll be willing to risk being cancelled by friends, family, employers, and more to advocate for righteousness in the public square?

Highly doubtful.

That's why the necessary first step in the ACT sequence is to know your authority.

Everyone has an authority in their life for determining what's true about reality, what's good or bad, right or wrong, harmful or helpful. But that doesn't mean everyone looks to the *right* authority. Research clearly shows that the vast majority of Americans—and even those who identify as Christians—look to themselves as their authority rather than God, as revealed through His Word.

Recall that in chapter 3, we learned that 65 percent of Americans self-identify as Christians, but according to the American World-view Inventory, only about 4 percent hold beliefs consistent with what the Bible teaches. To be clear, this doesn't mean 4 percent of respondents are able to answer a battery of challenging theological questions correctly. Researchers classify respondents as having a biblical worldview if only 80 percent of their answers line up with basic truths taught in the Bible (for example, the Bible is the accurate and reliable Word of God, absolute moral truth exists, God is all-knowing/all-loving/all-powerful, being "good" is insufficient for salvation, and so on).[1]

There's a huge gap between 65 percent of people identifying as Christians and 4 percent having a biblical worldview. I would call this an authority gap. It's the gap between those who merely identify as Christians and those who actually see reality through the lens of God's authoritative Word.

Some people fall in that gap because they intentionally reject biblical authority. Many in this group would knowingly identify as progressive Christians (see chapter 2). While they take the name of Christ, they have no objective basis for knowing anything about Him because they reject the Bible as God's Word. And if you don't believe God has revealed Himself in the Bible (or any other Scriptures), who will you look to as the authority on what's true? Yourself. Ultimately, then, progressive Christians look to the same authority as secular nonbelievers do.

Others in the gap do believe the Bible is God's Word but unknowingly hold unbiblical beliefs. This is a problem with biblical literacy. People in this group know who their rightful authority is, but they don't fully know or understand what He's said. *When this is the case, the functioning authority in a person's life is ironically still themself.* They may believe God is their authority and want God to be their authority, but their actual views end up being based on their own errant understanding.

Still others in the gap believe the Bible is God's Word and yet knowingly hold beliefs that aren't consistent with what it clearly teaches. This sounds counterintuitive, but there's plenty of cognitive dissonance that's happening in the body of Christ today due to secular pressures on our beliefs. For example, I've spoken with many people who would absolutely say they hold the Bible to be God's Word...but they don't believe that _____ (fill in the blank with an unpopular biblical position, frequently about gender or sexuality). It's basically an exception policy. They're willing to accept most everything, but on certain issues, they're going to go with their own understanding. People tend to be willing to do that because certain biblical teachings don't fit their preconceived notions about what God would say is good or bad, so they conclude that those teachings must somehow be in error.

What can we conclude after considering the nature of these three groups? *When it comes to matters of authority, most Christians are functional deists.*

As we saw in chapter 2, a deistic God is one who created the universe, never revealed Himself through any kind of Scripture, and doesn't interact with the world in any way. If the Creator were this kind of God, we would have no objective basis for knowing who He is, who we are, why we're here, what moral standards may exist, or anything else. Every person would necessarily be left to their own authority to determine what's true.

Statistically speaking, most Christians are at least functioning as though they live in a deistic universe of this nature—one without authoritative revelation. Whether they function in that way knowingly or not, the result is the same. Because they're unanchored from God's unchanging, objectively true Word, they're set adrift in a sea of confusion about the issues that matter most. They choose their way rather than God's way.

If we're going to persevere in a hostile public square, we must first collectively gain far more clarity on where our authority lies. When we unequivocally know that the Bible is our source for truth, we'll also unequivocally know that God has told us what is good for individuals and, by extension, communities. The confidence of knowing we're advocating for what God Himself wants is a powerful driver of perseverance.

So, how can we regain more clarity on our authority?

First, we need to better understand basic biblical apologetics. Apologetics is the study of why there's good reason to believe Christianity is true (1 Peter 3:15). Biblical apologetics more specifically is the study of why there's good reason to believe the Bible is true. Though I've never seen a research study on it, I'd guess that much of the hesitancy in the church around persevering in the public square on difficult issues comes from Christians not feeling sure that the Bible is actually God's Word. And that feeling may or may not be a conscious one. Some may be very aware of their questions, whereas others may simply have nagging doubts in the back of their mind. If either situation rings true for you, know that there are many excellent resources for gaining confidence in the reliability of the Bible. I've provided recommendations at this endnote.[2] If you're not confident that your source for truth is actually true, you won't be willing to persevere to share it in the face of hostility.

Second, we need to regain awe for what the Bible is. If you've been a longtime Christian, it can be easy to unintentionally trivialize in your mind the significance of the Bible being God's Word. The God who created the entire universe—in all of its incredible complexity and splendor—left us a book.[3] Do we really process that? When we look at how the heavens declare His glory (Psalm 19:1), do we marvel that the same God left us a guide on what we need to know about our entire existence? It's mind-boggling, if we aren't too jaded to realize the significance of that fact. An awe-filled reverence for the nature of the Bible is an important motivator for continually returning to Scripture as our authority.

Third, we need to better understand the implications of the Bible being God's Word. If the Bible is God's own Word, then its instructions are not only authoritative but are also *good* because they're given by our perfect Creator (Mark 10:18). When we don't understand the *why* behind certain teachings, we can sometimes be tempted to conclude that our own views are morally better, kinder, or more compassionate. *But you can't outdo God.* No matter how you may happen to feel, you simply aren't in a better position to determine what is true, good, and beautiful than the Creator of the universe. Truly recognizing the Bible's authority means being willing to trust what it says over your subjective feelings.

Strengthen Conviction

In an opinion column titled "Christians compelled to advocate for best transgender care," Lutheran Bishop Sue Briner and Episcopalian Bishop Suffragan Kai Ryan make the case that opposing gender transitions is a violation of human dignity:

> We faithfully hold the position that God calls us to meet the needs of transgender individuals and to empower them to flourish through the means of care which medical and therapeutic professionals continue to hold up as the gold standard. We stand with our transgender siblings and their parents and doctors, opposing interference with their access to medical and psychological care because it violates the human dignity we seek to uphold.[4]

In the prior section on knowing your authority, we talked about the necessity of going to the Bible as our source for knowing what's true. But what happens when Christians go to the Bible and then come to different conclusions? What happens when professing Christians like Briner and Ryan claim that helping those with gender dysphoria attempt gender transitions is a recognition of human dignity, while others claim that such attempts are a denial of the basic created order?

These kinds of questions prompt the next letter in the ACT sequence. Once we know our biblical authority, we must strengthen our conviction on the biblical positions we hold. In other words, we need the conviction that what we're advocating for is based on a right *understanding* of what God's authoritative Word teaches.

Unfortunately, there's increasing confusion on this today given the abundance of views we encounter, particularly online. Let's consider some ways this happens.

Sometimes Christians are confused by interactions with nonbelievers who aren't even making claims about what the Bible teaches. But confusion still happens because the language that culture uses to discuss controversial subjects is often designed to shame those who disagree into thinking they *must* be wrong. For example, if you disagree about the morality of homosexuality, you're labeled *homophobic*. To be phobic is to be irrationally afraid of something. I've never met a Christian who is afraid of gay people, much less irrationally so. I bet you haven't either. But the language is powerful. It implies that you hold your views out of fear, and it's enough to make some Christians question their position—even when they know what the Bible teaches and believe it's God's Word.

Culture's use of this kind of emotionally charged language is one glaring reason Christians are sometimes confused by nonbelievers, but in *Faithfully Different,* I discuss four more subtle presuppositions of culture that are also confusing many Christians today: 1) feelings are the ultimate guide; 2) happiness is the ultimate goal; 3) judging is the ultimate sin; and 4) God is the ultimate guess.[5] These cultural presuppositions about the nature of reality are far less overt in their conflict with Christianity than some of the language we just discussed. They've quietly diffused into the cultural air we breathe, and many Christians have unsuspectingly grafted them onto their biblical worldview even though they don't belong there. A Christian who has embraced these ideas may think, for example, *People should be happy and feel like their true selves, so I think Christians should support gender transitions.* This kind of reasoning, however, is based on culture's values and priorities rather than on biblical teachings; from a biblical perspective, a person's subjective happiness is *not* the ultimate goal of life (for more on regaining biblical clarity in a secular culture, see *Faithfully Different*).

While interactions with nonbelievers are often a source of confusion for Christians given what we just discussed, plenty of confusion also comes from people who identify as Christians. Consider the earlier quote from Briner and Ryan, leaders in their Lutheran and Episcopalian denominations. At least on a cursory level, their language might sound biblical. They refer to God calling us, they say they want to empower people to "flourish," and they state they want to uphold "human dignity." Saying they want to stand with their transgender siblings and parents sounds like a show of solidarity with fellow image bearers who are suffering. A Christian may believe they know what a clear biblical position is on the created order of biological sexes but end up second-guessing their understanding after reading statements like this one repeatedly over time.

There are a couple of important things to note here about confusion stemming from professing Christians. As we discussed previously, not everyone who identifies as a Christian holds the Bible to be God's authoritative Word. Just because someone appeals to biblical-sounding language doesn't mean they're even *attempting* to derive a position consistent with what the Bible teaches. In other cases, Christians may *think* they're deriving their position from the Bible, but they may be drawing unbiblical conclusions for any number of reasons. I don't know what Briner and Ryan's view of the Bible is, but it's not biblical to conclude that human flourishing and dignity can be upheld by affirming a person's feelings over the objective truth of God's created order (see chapter 9 for more on this). The bottom line is we must always remember that just because a person takes the name of Christ doesn't mean they hold biblical positions.

In light of all the confusion—whatever the source—what should we as Christians do to gain the conviction that comes from knowing our positions are truly consistent with God's Word?

First, we should be ever mindful that our views must be rooted in what Scripture itself says—not what culture says, not how we feel, and not what other Christians say. If we're not studying the Bible consistently and deeply, we're leaving ourselves to be more easily influenced by those who surround us than by God Himself. Bible study could not be a more important discipline. Now, that's not to imply that we should never consider what others say—sometimes it's fellow believers who help us *better* understand what the Bible teaches. But we should be like the Bereans in Acts 17:10-11, who tested all things against Scripture. That includes what your friends say, what your pastor says, what your small group leader teaches, what Christian authors write (yes, including me!), and everyone else.

Second, we need to understand the culture that surrounds us. I've encountered many Christians over time who recoil at this notion. They say, "I'm going to spend my time studying truth, not lies!" They then appeal to the oft-repeated idea that federal agents don't learn to spot counterfeit money by studying the counterfeits; they study genuine bills until they've mastered the real thing. The idea is that once you know truth, you'll automatically be adept at spotting falsehoods. This sounds good, but it's a poor analogy. There's a major difference between a small, concrete bill and something as large and complex as the underlying worldview of an entire culture. Seemingly innocuous yet unbiblical ideas (like happiness being the ultimate goal of life) are readily slipping past the biblical filter of many Christians today. It's not necessarily because they don't know truth, but because the falsehoods can be so deceptive.

A more relevant analogy to remember is that we would never go to a doctor who only studies healthy bodies and refuses to study disease. We know that keeping our bodies healthy requires a knowledge of what can and does go wrong. Taking the time to keep up with the news; following written, audio, or video sources that offer analyses of the news from a biblical worldview; and reading books to gain a deeper understanding of worldview subjects all go a long way toward increasing our knowledge of the diseased culture in which we're living today. Knowledge of the disease helps maintain clarity on health—conviction that your positions aren't unduly influenced by the world around you.

Third, take time to study objections to biblical views on controversial subjects. When *Roe v. Wade* was overturned by the US Supreme Court in June 2022, a flood of questions were asked in Christian Facebook groups about how to respond to a variety of criticisms nonbelievers were posting online about the decision. These questions were typically coming from Christians who held the Bible to be God's Word and had the conviction of knowing their pro-life position was consistent with what the Bible teaches, but they still felt unprepared to defend their view in light of some specific cultural objections (for example, the ever-popular claim that "no one has a right to tell a woman what she should or shouldn't do with her body"). The objections didn't necessarily shake their underlying convictions, but once they understood *how to respond*, their convictions deepened further. With this in mind, I've included responses to popular objections in each of the forthcoming chapters as well as recommendations for further study at the end of this book—all in the hope of strengthening readers' conviction on these issues.

We've now considered how perseverance is driven by 1) knowing your biblical authority and 2) strengthening conviction that what you're advocating for is based on a right understanding of what the Bible teaches. These two factors drive motivation and confidence, but both of them can also be weakened when there are particularly high costs to *acting* on them. And thus we come to the final and necessary step in the ACT sequence: maintain tenacity in the face of costly challenges.

Maintain Tenacity

In a *First Things* article titled "The Three Worlds of Evangelicalism," author Aaron Renn insightfully divides the story of America's changing religious landscape into three distinct stages. In the "positive world" (pre-1994), society largely retained a positive view of Christianity. Being a churchgoing person was part of being a good citizen, and publicly associating with Christianity was a status enhancer. In the "neutral world" (1994–2014), society began taking a more neutral stance toward Christianity. Christianity no longer held a privileged status in society, but it wasn't necessarily disfavored either. It was considered one valid option among many others in the public square. But everything shifted significantly around 2014. For the first time, American society came to have a distinctly *negative* view of Christianity. Renn characterizes this "negative world" in which we now find ourselves as follows:

> Being known as a Christian is a social negative, particularly in the elite domains of society. Christian morality is expressly repudiated and seen as a threat to the public good and the new public moral order. Subscribing to Christian moral views or violating the secular moral order brings negative consequences.[6]

This succinct statement describes the nature of our present situation quite well, especially the last sentence. We wouldn't even have to discuss the need to maintain tenacity if we weren't living in a culture where subscribing to Christian moral views or violating the secular moral order brings *negative consequences*. There are increasingly high costs to publicly acting on our convictions, and we must be prepared to navigate those costs in order to continue being obedient to the Lord.

In my experience, part of the difficulty in equipping Christians to prepare for the new negative world reality is that some in the church are still living in pockets of the *neutral* world and don't yet see the need for preparation. Even though Renn pegs 2014 as the year in which we transitioned to a negative world environment, societal shifts don't function like an on-off switch that causes everyone to see and experience changes at the same time. Renn notes, for example:

The pressures of the negative world are more intense in higher status and more elite domains, where secular ideologies most in conflict with Christianity are also most embedded. Because different evangelicals have differing degrees of exposure to this pressure, the shift to the negative world has put different types of levels of pressure on the different evangelical groups.[7]

Some of the factors that might determine the degree to which a Christian has been exposed to the negative world include where they live (rural versus urban area; conservative versus liberal state), their field of work or job function, their kids' educational experiences, the predominant views of close family members and friends, the degree to which their church community proactively addresses cultural topics, and their personal interest in and approach to following the news. For example, if you live in rural Nebraska, own a small restaurant in town, homeschool your kids, mostly associate with friends from church, have no family members who hold views hostile to Christianity, attend a church that doesn't apply the Bible to cultural topics, and have little interest in the news, you could easily come to the conclusion that things aren't *that* crazy for Christians today. Your life circumstances are collectively functioning like a neutral world pocket in the midst of a negative world society.

On the other end of the spectrum, if you live in Portland, Oregon, work for a large corporation that promotes secular social justice ideologies, have kids in public school, maintain friendships from widely varied areas of your life, have family members who believe Christianity is toxic, attend a church that addresses cultural issues, and follow the news closely, you have no doubt about the negative world reality. You experience it daily and often with great difficulty.

My point here is not that one set of circumstances is necessarily more desirable than the other—I'm not saying we all need to move to rural Nebraska! Rather, my point is that Christians have varied levels of exposure to the negative world reality, and those who experience fewer touchpoints with it need to know it's only a matter of time before they'll experience it in greater ways. So, whether you currently have significant or little negative world exposure, it's important to understand the costs we must be prepared to persevere through as culture becomes increasingly hostile to Christianity. I'll highlight here two kinds of costs that Christians are already facing to significant degrees: the cost of relationships and the cost of financial security.

The Cost of Relationships

In the positive and neutral worlds, Christians in America rarely faced a pattern of relational costs due to their faith, but in the negative world, that's rapidly changing. There's not a conference at which I speak where I don't talk to multiple believers expressing their deep grief over the family and friend relationships they've lost in the last few years due to being a Christian. Especially pained are the parents whose adult kids have cut them off for holding what they consider to be toxic beliefs (typically about gender and sexuality).

In a Facebook group I manage, I recently asked if anyone had personal experiences they would be willing to share about being "canceled" by people in their lives over their faith. Several dozen heartbreaking stories were immediately posted, followed by a stream of private emails. Here are just a few brief examples of the kinds of things people shared:

- "I have so many stories of friends and family canceling me because of my faith that I could write a book, each chapter as sad as the one before."

- "My brother deleted me on Facebook because of my views on abortion and LGBTQ. We are actually no-contact now."

- "I have no relationship with my eldest sister and parents because I refuse to put my children in a secular school, opting instead to home-educate them in order to instill a biblical worldview."

- "The hardest part for me is when being canceled by friends and family really impacted my kids. Their relationships with friends and classmates have definitely been changed. They have experienced being excluded from friends' circles because of what I have believed and spoken up about."

- "Three family members unfriended me for my biblically based views on sexuality and one sister refused to speak to me."

- "My cousin blocks family members on Facebook when they say something she doesn't like. One example is she blocked me because I put a sad face on pictures she posted of her at a pro-choice rally."

- "My younger sister has stopped coming to holiday and family gatherings because we do not affirm her decision to live with her girlfriend."

Again, this is just a tiny sampling of stories shared with me on a single day. In recent years, many Christians have felt the shock of people breaking off relationships so readily, but Jesus warned us this would happen. In Luke 12:51-53, He says:

> Do you think that I have come to give peace on earth? No, I tell you, but rather division. For from now on in one house there will be five divided, three against two and two against three. They will be divided, father against son and son against father, mother against daughter and daughter against mother, mother-in-law against her daughter-in-law and daughter-in-law against mother-in-law.

The fact that Jesus told us to expect divisions from those closest to us doesn't make this any easier. There is deep pain that accompanies many of these losses. But this does tell us that Jesus expects us to be faithful to Him over anyone else and that we shouldn't be surprised when our fidelity results in relational loss. Our love for God and our love for others in not shying away from truth must come first.

The Cost of Financial Security

Christians are also facing increasing challenges in the workplace today as organizations and entire industries are shifting to policies and work environments that require Christians to affirm and act on ideologies at fundamental odds with their faith. As just a few examples:

- Public schoolteachers are required to teach and affirm LGBTQ materials, use students' chosen pronouns, and instruct from a secular social justice perspective.

- People working in corporations are required to attend Diversity, Equity, and Inclusion (DEI) trainings, affirm DEI conclusions, and execute those conclusions in the workplace (DEI is typically based on the secular social justice philosophy we'll discuss in chapter 7).

- Medical and mental health professionals are required to adhere to treatment guidelines at odds with their convictions (for example, the unquestioned affirmation of a patient's desire to change genders).

- Prospective job applicants are required to signal their acceptance of secular ideologies in order to even be *considered* for the job (as one job posting shared with me put it, applicants must have a "willingness and commitment to include equity, social justice, and inclusion in all practices").

Job challenges are extending to entrepreneurs as well. For example, one man shared with me, "My wife and I own a small café, and people from the community attempted to cancel us and our business because I showed up to a pride event with a white board [and this] question written on it: 'Does Any God Exist?'" That's all it took for people to want to cancel their business—asking a question about the existence of God. Entrepreneurs who in any way express their beliefs publicly can expect to be targeted and canceled by those who consider Christianity to be toxic.

There are no easy answers for what Christians should do when confronted with these types of challenges. In some cases, pushback may be welcomed in the name of religious freedom and Christians may be able to find a workable solution without leaving or losing their job. In other cases, particularly when entire fields are moving in one direction, Christians may find it impossible to hold firmly to their convictions while remaining in their positions. Whatever the case may be, believers must at the very least be prepared to make hard decisions that will result in significant financial loss.

In light of substantial and often painful costs like those I've highlighted here, how can we maintain tenacity? How can we keep going, no matter the cost? It starts with a major reset of our expectations: *Being a Christian will cost you.* Christians have been comfortable for hundreds of years in America and haven't had to grapple much with the costs that Jesus Himself told us would come, but everything is changing now. If we expect comfort to continue despite the major worldview shift underlying our culture, we are fooling ourselves. Our mindset must change if we're going to be prepared to persevere through potentially great costs.[8]

If maintaining tenacity starts with resetting our expectations, it ends with continually being mindful that we're accountable to God, not man. Man may break relationships and man may take away jobs—man may even take away our very life—but someday we will stand in awe before God and answer for the choices we made during our short existence on Earth. When we remember we're accountable to God and not man, we'll be spurred toward the boldness needed to push through costly challenges in the name of all that is good and true. May we all make tenacious decisions resulting in the King of kings saying, "Well done, good and faithful servant" (Matthew 25:23)!

■ ■ ■

As we transition now to part 2, I hope you'll give thoughtful consideration to how each of the forthcoming and highly promi-nent issues is worth persevering for in the public square, even in the midst of hate. Again, these aren't the only significant issues on which Christians are disdained for their views, but they're some of the ones believers most urgently need to consider. I pray that the following chapters will equip you to more deeply understand culture's mental-ity so you can better respond in truth and love for the glory of God and the good of others.

CHAPTER 5 SUMMARY

- Godly perseverance in a hostile culture requires knowing your (biblical) <u>a</u>uthority, strengthening <u>c</u>onviction, and maintaining <u>t</u>enacity (which can be remembered through the ACT acronym).

- Knowing our <u>a</u>uthority means recognizing that the Bible is our source for truth because it's God's own Word.

- Strengthening your <u>c</u>onviction means gaining the confidence that what you're advocating for is based on a right understanding of what God's Word teaches.

- Maintaining <u>t</u>enacity means being willing to tirelessly act on your convictions, even in the face of increasingly high personal costs.

PART 2:

RESPONDING TO AND PERSEVERING THROUGH TODAY'S MOST PROMINENT CHARGES

CHAPTER 6

DANGEROUS CHRISTIAN NATIONALISTS

The View from the Mainstream Media[1]

■ ■ ■

The first headline I saw on the news this morning was the following one from MSNBC.com: "Christian nationalists are a small and dangerous group with outsized power."[2] Clicking on the link revealed the following subtitle: "New data from the Public Religion Research Institute reveals which pockets of the country have become hotbeds for extremely theocratic views." The Public Religion Research Institute's site itself featured the ominous headline, "Support for Christian Nationalism in All 50 States."[3]

Extreme. Theocratic. Pervasive. If it weren't for the fact that this was just the latest in a decade-long trail of media warnings about Christian nationalism, it would have sounded like something new and horrible was happening. In reality, the media has been sounding an alarm for several years now that Christian nationalism is one of the greatest and most terrifying threats to American democracy. And I do mean that quite literally. Author Katherine Stewart wrote, for example, in *The New York Times*, "The shape of the Christian nationalist movement in the post-Roe future is coming into view, and it should terrify anyone concerned for the future of constitutional democracy…Breaking American democracy isn't an unintended side effect of Christian nationalism. It is the point of the project."[4]

In spite of the media's constant and ever-growing attention to this subject, research shows that 54 percent of Americans have never even heard of Christian nationalism.[5] If you're one of them, don't feel bad. Even those who *have* heard of it don't know what it is. No one does—including the media.

What Is Christian Nationalism?

In saying no one knows what Christian nationalism is, I'm being slightly facetious—but only slightly. A more accurate statement would be that everyone who uses the term has their own (often unstated) ideas of what it means, those ideas are often vastly different in nature from the ones underlying others' understanding of the term, and there's no commonly accepted definition to which anyone can appeal. Sociologists differ in their definitions, media outlets differ in their definitions, politicians differ in their definitions, and theologians differ in their definitions—as does everyone else.

That said, we've got to start somewhere, so a broad common denominator *tends* to be the idea that Christian nationalism is a problematic merging of Christian and American identities. For example, sociologists Samuel Perry and Andrew Whitehead define Christian nationalism as a "cultural framework that blurs distinctions between Christian identity and American identity, viewing the two as closely related and seeking to enhance and preserve their union."[6]

If you feel like you're no closer to understanding what, exactly, Christian nationalism is, you're seeing the challenge. What does it mean to "merge" identities or "blur distinctions," and for whom is it problematic? Does it mean there are Christians who are placing a love for country over a love for God? Does it mean there are Christians who believe America was founded on predominantly Christian values and seek to maintain a society based on those values? Does it mean that there are Christians who believe they're called to influence today's public square based on their convictions? Does it mean there are Christians who want to make Christianity an established state church (contra the First Amendment)? As we'll see in this chapter, it could mean any of those things *and many more*, depending on who's using the term.[7]

So, here's where we are: The media continually warns about the threat of Christian nationalism (thus making it an important subject to include in this book), but no one defines the threat in the same way. That means our task in this chapter is quite challenging. We can't simply evaluate *one* issue here—Christian nationalism—because that term represents a plethora of distinct issues. Some of those issues are problematic, and some aren't. What we'll do in this chapter is look at both sociological research and media coverage to parse out and evaluate the most common individual concerns that arise under the Christian nationalism banner. There are certainly other types of concerns sometimes raised—we can't cover absolutely everything here—but the ensuing discussion represents a lion's share of the conversation related to the subject of this book.

For those who don't love data, I apologize in advance that we need to dig into some research now. But you can't understand this subject without understanding the data. And because culture thinks something that at least some Christians are doing is one of the *biggest threats to our country today*, we need to take the time to understand and respond to the charges.

What the Research Shows

While we obviously don't have the space to look at every study that has ever attempted to measure some aspect of what people might call *Christian nationalism*, we're going to look at the two largest and most frequently cited studies in recent years.

Whitehead and Perry

In 2020, sociologists Andrew L. Whitehead and Samuel L. Perry wrote a highly influential book called *Taking America Back for God: Christian Nationalism in the United States* based primarily on their analysis of the 2017 Baylor Religion Survey.[8] Because it's been referenced so many times in the media as evidence for the problems with Christian nationalism, it's important to understand the nature of their work. Foreword writer Robert P. Jones, the CEO and founder of the Public Religion Research Institute, calls this "one of the clearest portraits we have of the greatest existing threat to democracy in our fraught contemporary moment."[9]

Whitehead and Perry evaluated respondents' orientation toward Christian nationalism according to their levels of agreement or disagreement with the following six statements:

1. The federal government should declare the United States a Christian nation.

2. The federal government should advocate Christian values.

3. The federal government should enforce strict separation of church and state.

4. The federal government should allow the display of religious symbols in public spaces.

5. The success of the United States is part of God's plan.

6. The federal government should allow prayer in public schools.[10]

The first statement is at least *fairly* clear (implying support for some kind of formal relationship between the US and Christianity that doesn't presently exist), but there are serious questions that may be raised regarding the meaning of the other statements to any given respondent. For example, what does it mean for the government to "advocate Christian values"? After all, prohibiting rape is one of many values consistent with Christianity, and no one seems to have a problem with the government making laws accordingly. As we discussed in chapter 4, *all* public policy involves someone's values being imposed on someone else.

Similarly, what does "strict" separation of church and state mean, given that even the Supreme Court has differed in its interpretation of that boundary over time? What kinds of religious symbols would we be talking about, and would they be limited to Christian symbols only? What does it mean for US success to be part of God's plan as opposed to anything else, given that all things are ultimately under God's sovereignty? And what kind of allowance for prayer in public schools is meant here—who would be leading, when, and under what circumstances?

Despite these highly problematic ambiguities, Whitehead and Perry classified respondents into four groups based on their presumed views of Christian nationalism: Rejectors (21.5 percent), Resisters (26.6 percent), Accommodators (32.1 percent), and Ambassadors (19.8 percent). Yes, according to this classification, over half of Americans are to some degree "Christian nationalists" (the Accommodators and Ambassadors).[11]

Whitehead and Perry go on in the rest of their book to show how Christian nationalists, by their definition, differ in demographics and responses to a variety of questions relative to Rejectors and Resisters. Their analyses and questions are far from being ideologically neutral. For example, they identify the following as one of the most "pressing national questions" they seek to understand: "Why do Americans advocate so vehemently for xenophobic policies, such as a border wall with Mexico?"[12] Regardless of what one thinks about a border wall, it's fair to say that there are many reasons people differ on immigration policies and controls other than xenophobia (an irrational fear or hatred of people from other countries).

Examples like this exist on nearly every page, but here's one more to give you an idea of how Whitehead and Perry's Christian nationalism is hardly distinguishable from a broad conservativism. The following statements are shown on a chart as examples of how Christian nationalists problematically skew differently in their views from Rejectors and Resisters:[13]

- "Federal government should enact stricter gun laws"

- "Abortion is always wrong, even if the family cannot afford the child"

- "Middle East refugees are a terror threat"

- "Government spending too little on the military, armaments, and defense"

- "People should be made to show respect for America's traditions"

So, if a person thinks existing gun laws are sufficient, believes abortion is always wrong, has concerns that refugees from the Middle East could pose a threat of terrorism, is in favor of increased national defense, and thinks that certain American traditions warrant some kind of required respect from citizens, that's an inherently problematic set of views associated with a *dangerous Christian nationalism*. This is just one set of questions from many in the book with a similar ideological bent.

We'll return to more of Whitehead and Perry's analysis later in this chapter.

Public Religion Research Institute

The Public Religion Research Institute (PRRI) surveyed more than 22,000 Americans in 2023 on Christian nationalism as part of its

American Values Atlas—what PRRI says is the "largest dataset ever assembled on this topic."[14] To measure Christian nationalism, PRRI researchers asked respondents to rate their level of agreement or disagreement with the following five statements:

1. The U.S. government should declare America a Christian nation.

2. Laws should be based on Christian values.

3. If the U.S. moves away from our Christian foundations, we will not have a country anymore.

4. Being Christian is an important part of being truly American.

5. God has called Christians to exercise dominion over all areas of American society.[15]

Questions 1 and 2 are very similar to those used in Whitehead and Perry's book (with the corresponding problems previously noted on question 2). Questions 3-5 are different, but yet again, we find that they're highly ambiguous. Still, researchers classified respondents based on their answers and found that 10 percent are "Christian nationalism adherents" (overwhelmingly agreeing or completely agreeing with the statements) and 19 percent are "Christian nationalism sympathizers" (agree with the statements but are less likely to completely agree). From PRRI's perspective, then, about 29 percent of Americans are in some sense Christian nationalists.

Like Whitehead and Perry, PRRI researchers go on to show how Christian nationalists differ in demographics and responses to a variety of questions relative to non-Christian nationalists. And also like Whitehead and Perry, there is very much an ideological bent to their questions and analyses. For example, in a section of their report in which they identify the "Issue Priorities of Christian Nationalists," they cite five issues that function as a "litmus test" for how Christian nationalists vote: access to guns, immigration, abortion, LGBTQ issues, and climate change. And once again, the positions on these issues that are typically considered to be conservative are part of the researchers' profile of what's "problematic" about Christian nationalists.

We'll return to PRRI's findings later in this chapter as well.

Key Takeaways from the Research

Here's the bottom line to remember from these two prominent and influential studies on Christian nationalism:

- Researchers use a highly ambiguous set of questions to determine people's orientation toward what they think of as Christian nationalism.

- The people who end up grouped as Christian nationalists based on the way these questions are framed tend to be conservative Christians.

- Researchers then show how this group of Christian nationalists (who are, for the most part, merely conservative Christians) hold views unpopular with progressives and presuppose that's indicative of a pervasive problem.

This quick summary explains why culture broadly has such disdain for Christian nationalism—it tends to have disdain for anyone who holds conservative positions. But why are these disdained positions considered *dangerous* per se? For that answer, we need to understand the media's narrative.

The Media's "Dangerous" Narrative

While there's a relatively limited number of major research studies on Christian nationalism to survey, media coverage of the subject is extensive. At the time of this writing, a Google search on the term, for example, turns up 2.3 million results, and there's no easy way to identify and quantify the widely varied concerns about Christian nationalism that all those pieces of content are raising. However, after surveying hundreds of them to identify the specific types of concerns they cite, it's clear that those concerns are overwhelmingly of three types: 1) Christians imposing (conservative) values on others through the political process, 2) racism, or 3) xenophobia.

Imposition of (Conservative) Values

Much, if not most, of the media's concern with Christian nationalism mirrors the concerns of the researchers discussed previously: Those whom they call *Christian nationalists* advocate for policies associated with culturally disdained conservative positions. Sometimes the media refers to researchers' definition of Christian nationalists, but oftentimes they presuppose their own definition that boils down to the following logic:

- Christians who vote in politically conservative ways want to impose their religiously informed (and unpopular) views on everyone else.

- Religiously informed views aren't supposed to be brought into the public square in a "secular" democracy.

- These people are therefore antidemocratic and/or theocratic and pose a dangerous threat to our pluralistic democracy.

- We'll call them *Christian nationalists* for wanting to impose *Christian* values on the whole *nation* when a pluralistic society holds many different beliefs.

There are two underlying assumptions here that render the entire narrative wrong-minded: 1) that it's an antidemocratic imposition of values for any given segment of people to advocate for their views in the public square, and 2) that it's theocratic if a person or group advocates for views that are religiously informed.

Let's briefly revisit two key points from chapter 4 in response.

First, in *every* matter of policy, someone is imposing their view on someone else; it's no more imposing of one group to advocate for a policy rooted in their values than it is for a group with an opposing position to advocate for a policy rooted in theirs. Ironically, advocating for policies based on your views isn't antidemocratic—it's using our democracy exactly as it's intended to be used! (For the record, the United States is technically a constitutional federal republic, but I'm using the colloquial terminology of democracy here because that's the language typically used by the media).[16] To be antidemocratic would be to seek another form of government or to attempt to skirt proper procedures *within* our current system. Neither of these things is happening when people simply advocate for policies according to their values.

Second, to be secular only means the United States is not committed to the authority of any particular religion in public life. Individuals, however, are free to advocate for policies that follow from their convictions—religious or otherwise. Advocating for views that happen to be religiously informed is therefore not theocratic. A theocracy is an entirely different form of government, in which God or a deity is formally recognized as the supreme civil ruler. Calling Christians who advocate for their religiously informed views theocratic may make for powerful rhetoric, but it's a sloppy and inaccurate use of language. Additionally, if no one could advocate for views of morality based on biblical or other religious teachings, we would have virtually no laws. Nearly everyone wants laws against behaviors like rape, murder, and theft, but laws like these would have to be eliminated on such a principle.

All of that said, it's questionable to assume the media doesn't understand this—*because they don't label it Christian nationalism if a*

Christian's convictions lead him or her to advocate for progressive positions. It seems clear that their concern isn't actually with religiously motivated positions seeking a theocracy of some kind, but rather, with Christians advocating for conservative policies that run contrary to the popular moral consensus. Professor Mark David Hall summarizes the double standard well:

> A major problem with much of the literature on Christian nationalism is that it is profoundly subjective, often amounting to little more than a critique that Christians are motivated by their faith to seek an end critics dislike. So, for instance, to be motivated by one's faith to seek to end abortion is Christian nationalism, whereas to be motivated by one's faith to end segregation is praiseworthy.[17]

Consider, for example, an article from *The Guardian* titled "US set for flurry of 'Christian nationalist' bills advanced by religious right," with the subtitle "Legislation that would erode LGBTQ and reproductive rights expected to be introduced in states across America, experts warn."[18] The article's specific examples of bills considered to be Christian nationalist in nature include anything restricting abortion, preventing trans people from using bathrooms that don't correspond with their biological sex, and limiting adoption for same-sex couples. These are all questions of public policy that should rightly be a matter of debate in a democracy. But because conservative positions on these issues are culturally unpopular, the corresponding bills are pejoratively labeled *Christian nationalist.*

As another example, in an article on ABCNews.com titled "'Christian nationalism' threatens democracy, some experts say," journalist Oren Oppenheim writes, "Although the full extent of the movement is unclear, experts who spoke with ABC News warned that the ideology of Christian nationalism threatens American democracy. They said it could lead to politicians passing laws that supporters believe reflect specific Christian values…"[19] Note again the presupposed problem with "specific Christian values," as though some groups' values are off the table for consideration in a democracy.

Similarly, consider comments from Politico reporter Heidi Przybyla. In an MSNBC interview, Przybyla said that the one thing that unites Christian nationalists is that "they believe that our rights as Americans as all human beings don't come from any earthly authority, they don't come from congress, they don't come from the Supreme Court, they come from God. The problem with that is that they are determining, [men] are determining what God is telling them…now you have an extremist element of conservative Christians who say that this applies specifically to issues including abortion, gay marriage, and it's going much further than that."[20]

It's not Christian nationalists who believe rights come from God, it's all Christians. If any inherent human rights exist, they *necessarily* come from a God with the authority and ability to give them. But regardless of where rights come from or where people even *think* their rights come from, it's obvious that Przybyla has a problem with "conservative Christians" applying their religious convictions to public policy—that's "extremist."

These are just a few examples that could be multiplied across all kinds of media content. The central takeaway is that when the media sounds alarms about Christian nationalism, much of the time their concerns are *false* alarms; they're not actual problems from either a biblical or civic perspective.

Racism

Another theme of media coverage on Christian nationalism centers on what is sometimes labeled *white* Christian nationalism: the idea that Christian nationalists are racist and dangerously want to see their racist views reflected in how society functions.

The media uses all kinds of anecdotal evidence to suggest racism among those they label *Christian nationalists*—some of which indicates actual racism (for example, explicit statements from self-identified white supremacist groups) and some of which does not (for example, Christians rejecting Critical Race Theory-based initiatives—see chapter 7). The widely varied nature of these anecdotes makes it impossible to analyze them in aggregate, but we can certainly say this: Where actual racism exists, Christians should be the first to unequivocally condemn it. Racism is entirely incompatible with the truth that God made every human in His image, equally and inherently valuable (Genesis 1:27).

But aside from individual anecdotes, is there quantifiable evidence of racism among those whom researchers have identified as Christian nationalists? That is certainly the assumption in much media coverage. And, indeed, the PRRI study came to conclusions that Christian nationalists have white supremacist tendencies, so let's look at that research.[21]

PRRI researchers asked respondents to rate their level of agreement or disagreement with the following statements to determine what they call "anti-black sentiment":

- Generations of slavery and discrimination have created conditions that make it difficult for many Black Americans to work their way out of the lower class.

- Today discrimination against white Americans has become as big a problem as discrimination against Black Americans and other minorities.

- A Black person is more likely to receive the death penalty for the same crime.

- White supremacy is still a major problem in the U.S. today.[22]

Because those whom PRRI classified as Christian nationalists skewed differently on their answers to these questions relative to non-Christian nationalists, researchers concluded it was evidence of antiblack racism.

But allow me to point out the obvious: *A person's views on these statements have no necessary relationship to racism.*

They simply measure people's perceptions of the degree to which white supremacy and discrimination remain a problem today. People can disagree in that perception without it reflecting *racism*. In fact, those who were identified as Christian nationalists skewed differently on their answers to these questions regardless of their race![23]

Racism can certainly still be found in America, and where it exists, it must be strongly condemned. But based on research, there's little reason to conclude that rightly defined racism dangerously characterizes some large group of people researchers have labeled *Christian nationalists*.

Xenophobia

Closely related to concerns about Christian nationalism being racist are concerns about it being xenophobic. The media narrative tends to be that those identified as Christian nationalists are fearful of immigrants because they believe immigration will lead to undesirable cultural change; Christian nationalists want to conserve a primarily European, Protestant culture that they associate with America's founding ideals.

The media's anecdotal evidence for this tends to be that those whom they label *Christian nationalists* are in favor of stricter forms of immigration control than progressives typically are, and the media subsequently assigns a motive for holding those beliefs (fear of losing cultural dominance). Researchers take a similar view. For example, Whitehead and Perry say, "Because support for Christian nationalism...favors boundaries of all sorts and especially national boundaries, it naturally breeds xenophobia (by which we mean an irrational fear or antipathy regarding immigrants that leads one to exclude them from group membership)."[24] So, if you believe national boundaries of some kind are necessary, that's apparently part of being a *xenophobic* Christian nationalist.

Similarly, PRRI researchers assessed what they call *anti-immigrant* attitudes by asking respondents to rate their level of agreement or disagreement with the following statements:

- The American way of life needs to be protected from foreign influence.

- The growing number of newcomers from other countries strengthens American society.

- Immigrants are invading our country and replacing our cultural and ethnic background.[25]

These statements reflect people's varied views on the amount and impact of immigration. But you would be hard-pressed to conclude from responses to these statements that someone is xenophobic, with the *possible* exception of the third one. The language "invading" has strong connotations, but that said, even the most progressive media outlets have been covering what has widely been described as a border crisis. Pew Research shows that 80 percent of Americans think the government is doing a "somewhat bad" or "very bad" job of "dealing with the large number of migrants seeking to enter the U.S. at the border with Mexico"—including a strong majority of both political parties.[26] If someone surveyed is comfortable labeling the situation an *invasion*, it doesn't necessarily mean they're xenophobic. It may just mean they have a concern about the impact of uncontrolled immigration on both would-be migrants and those already here (for example, national security, sex trafficking, economic strains, crime, and national debt).

Just as with racism, there are surely people in America who hold truly hostile, ungodly views toward people from other countries. And where that exists, it too should be strongly condemned. But most of the research questions used to profile Christian nationalists as xenophobic merely reflect differing opinions on immigration policy and the impact of immigration on culture—not an irrational and dangerous fear of others.

So, Does Christian Nationalism Threaten Democracy?

In any given piece of media coverage on Christian nationalism, you'll find a unique mix of claims about what Christian nationalism entails and why it's a problem—which is inevitable when there's no standard definition of the term. In some cases, they cite examples that Christians should absolutely condemn. We discussed two such examples in this chapter: *rightly defined* racism and *rightly defined* xenophobia. You can also find plenty of examples of individuals quoted who have a confused understanding of the proper constitutional relationship between church and state and photos of people holding signs with cringeworthy statements. These individual examples, however, do not characterize wide swaths of the population that researchers and the media otherwise label *Christian nationalists*.

One of the reasons this subject has become so confusing for Christians is that media coverage often mixes problematic examples with unproblematic examples, labels the whole package *Christian nationalism*, and drives the impression that there are large groups of Christians who hold beliefs dangerous to democracy—sometimes additionally referencing research data from highly ambiguous questions to supposedly prove their point.

The result is that many Christians have come to believe there's something inherently problematic about advocating for righteousness in the public square. The media has intimidated us into thinking we shouldn't "mix" our faith and political views—that if we bring our religiously informed values into the public square, we're problematically blurring distinctions between our Christian and American identities. Spiritually speaking, you *can* problematically put your identity in something other than Christ, but make no mistake: The media doesn't care about your spiritual health. When they're worried about you conflating your Christian and American identities, they're worried about you imposing unpopular values on others. As we've seen, they'll call that dangerously antidemocratic and theocratic, but it's neither. It's advocating for your views exactly as is intended within a democracy.

As American Christians, we should be grateful we live under a form of government that gives us the opportunity to advocate freely for the common good out of our love for both God and others. Don't relinquish that God-given opportunity just because the media wants you to fear being part of a "dangerous" movement. Remember that oftentimes the danger *they* fear is being legally restrained by policies rooted in what is objectively right according to God Himself.

Let them call that dangerous. We'll continue to call it good.

QUICK RESPONSES TO 5 POPULAR CHALLENGES
on Christian Nationalism

In each chapter of part 2, I'll provide quick (three sentences or fewer!) responses to five of the most popular challenges related to that chapter's subject, written in a way you can use to respond directly to someone making these and similar claims. Additionally, I'll preface each answer with important clarifying questions that you would ideally want to ask before responding. Because I don't have answers to those questions from your hypothetical challenger, my own responses are necessarily broad. My hope is that you'll find these sample answers helpful as starting points for tailoring replies to the specifics of your own conversations.

1. Christian nationalism is one of the biggest threats to democracy today.

(Questions: What do you mean by Christian nationalism? How do you see it threatening democracy?)

Christian nationalism has come to mean a lot of different things to different people—some of which I would consider to be problematic and some of which I wouldn't. But very few people mean something by it that's actually opposed to a democratic form of government. Oftentimes, people just mean that if Christians advocate for policies according to their values, that's in some way more problematic than when other people advocate for policies according to their values.

2. Christians want to set up a theocracy by imposing their values on everyone else.

(Questions: What do you mean by theocracy? What kinds of values do you think Christians are imposing on others in a way that's not consistent with a democratic form of government?)

Voting according to your religious convictions is in no way comparable to seeking a completely different form of government—a theocracy—in which a deity is recognized as the ruler. In a democracy, everyone is welcome to vote according to their moral convictions, regardless of whether they happen to be religiously motivated or not. In *every* matter of public policy, someone's views will be imposed on someone else.

3. Christians shouldn't be able to impose their values on everyone else because America has a separation of church and state.

(Questions: What, from your perspective, does separation of church and state mean? What is your basis for defining it that way? Can you share some examples of how you believe Christians are not respecting that boundary?)

The Establishment Clause of the First Amendment ensures that the government will not establish a state-supported church and will not force individuals to practice a specific religion; it's in that way that the church and state are to be separate. That has nothing to do, however, with how individuals should or should not use their religious beliefs to inform their participation in the political process.

4. America was never a Christian nation and shouldn't be today.

(Questions: What do you mean by Christian nation? What are some examples you see of people advocating for America to be a Christian nation in that way today?)

It's true that America never had a federally established state church, but most people also aren't advocating for that to change today. Christians advocate for their values in the public square just like any other citizen, but that doesn't mean we're seeking to make Christianity an established national religion in some way. It just means we're participating in the democratic process that already exists.

5. Christians just want power.

(Questions: Do you think it's inherently bad for a group to want power? Are there some who should be allowed to seek power and some who shouldn't? What makes Christians different from anyone else who wants to seek political office or influence?)

In any country with an established government, someone will be in power, and those in power had to seek that power. So, there's no reason to chastise any particular group for seeking the power necessary for public influence. Christians with political power, like anyone else, should steward that power well in advocating for the common good.

ACTIONS FOR THE COMMON GOOD:
7 Ways to Shine Your Light Through
Political Involvement

In each chapter of part 2, I'll also provide seven ideas for influencing the public square related to the chapter's subject. These lists are in no way exhaustive. They're merely meant to help you begin thinking about ways to advocate for the common good.

1. **Educate yourself on issues of political relevance for Christians.** For example, take advantage of the recommendations for further study provided at the end of this book. Stay up to date on current events related to important issues by subscribing to newsletters, reading news, or listening to podcasts that cover current events from a biblical worldview perspective. This knowledge will inform a host of possible next steps for action.

2. **Get to know who your Representatives and Senators are in both the US and state governments.** You can find your US congressmembers at the link in this endnote (state governments have individual websites you can find through a search engine).[27] Spend time on their websites to learn what issues they're involved in and sign up for email or text updates. Contact your congresspeople as needed to advocate for biblically informed positions.

3. **Vote.** This should go without saying, but all citizens should take advantage of the right to vote. Take the time to be informed about each issue and candidate on a ballot.

4. **Follow, donate to, and pray for Christian legal advocacy groups.** Groups like the Alliance Defending Freedom, the

American Center for Law and Justice, and the Pacific Justice Institute work to protect religious freedom, free speech, marriage and family, parental rights, and the sanctity of life. Follow organizations like these on social media to stay current on legal battles, pray for God-honoring outcomes, and donate. If you don't have social media, you can sign up for email updates through the organizations' individual websites.

5. **Support a nonprofit organization that advocates politically for specific issues.** If there's an issue that you're passionate about, search online for organizations that exist to educate on and advocate for that issue. Such organizations tend to offer a wide variety of ways to support their cause.

6. **Know and get involved with your local school board.** In the vast majority of cases, school board members are elected. They're accountable to the community and make critically important decisions about policies affecting every public school in their district. Learn who your board members are, follow their meetings, sign up to speak on issues as needed, or consider running for a position yourself.

7. **Help equip those in your church community with a better understanding of the role of public Christian influence.** Unfortunately, Christians have many negative preconceived notions about political involvement (such as the objections we covered in part 1). But if we, the body of Christ, better understood political involvement as just one way we can advocate for the common good out of our love for God and others, imagine how much more impact we could have in society! An easy way to get more people in your church thinking about important issues is by forming a group to

read and discuss a book together. Consider using a book like this one as a starting point, or dive into a book on a specific issue.

CHAPTER 7

POWER-HUNGRY OPPRESSORS

The View from Secular Social Justice Activists

■ ■ ■

In response to "questionable sociological, psychological, and political theories" making inroads into the church under the label of *social justice*, a group of high-profile pastors and other ministry leaders wrote a widely publicized document in 2018 called the Dallas Statement (also known as The Statement on Social Justice and the Gospel).[1] The writers sought to clarify biblical positions on race, gender, and sexuality, given the degree to which culture's ideas of social justice were confusing Christians on these issues.

Progressive author John Pavlovitz responded with a blog post mocking the creators and signers of the Dallas Statement.[2] Writing from their supposed perspective, he ridiculed their motivations, saying:

> We are terrified.
>
> We are afraid of gay people and Transgender people and brown people and Muslims—in a time when others are rapidly abandoning such fear.
>
> We are white, Conservative, old men, and we realize that we are rapidly dying dinosaurs approaching extinction.
>
> We see the culture becoming more intelligent, more scientifically aware, more connected across faith traditions

and borders, and far less willing to be dictated to by white, Conservative, old men—and we are panicking…

We want a Christianity that secures our privilege, that hordes our power, that doesn't require us to be at all confronted or inconvenienced by Jesus.

We will do anything to resist equality, curb diversity, and keep marginalized people where they are—even betray the very heart of the Gospels.

If you're not familiar with the dominant philosophy that underlies secular social justice thinking today, this excerpt should raise a lot of questions. What does being white have to do with views being right or wrong? What does it mean to secure the "privilege" of Christianity? Why is there an assumption that Christians want to hoard power? Why would biblical positions on race, gender, and sexuality imply to anyone that Christians want to "resist equality, curb diversity, and keep marginalized people where they are"?

While the answers to these questions may not be obvious on the surface, they'll become so by the end of this chapter (and we'll revisit them then). The assumptions and charges made by Pavlovitz follow a pattern of popular secular social justice thinking rooted in a philosophy called critical theory.[3] As we'll soon see, those who adhere to this philosophy don't merely think Christian views of justice are wrong. *Christians are seen as oppressors who use power to keep marginalized people down.* We're allegedly perpetrators of great *injustice*, worthy of the strongest condemnation.

How did we get to a point where Christians are known for (alleged) injustice rather than justice? Well, that takes a bit of explaining.

Good News: We All Agree on Something

There are relatively few statements that garner near-universal agreement in our increasingly polarized culture. But I've got one for you:

There are a lot of injustices in the world, and humans have a responsibility to do something about it.

Justice, therefore, is an interesting topic because you don't have to convince most people that it matters. Regardless of one's worldview, people everywhere realize that the world really is a desperately broken place. For example, an atheist asked on the website Quora, "If there are gods, why is the world so full of pain and injustice?"[4] Almost 100 people offered a reply, and not one challenged the underlying assumption of the question—that the world is indeed full of injustice. Everyone simply offered different explanations for that presumed reality. One atheist commented:

> God does not exist. We are the inevitable consequence of an expanding universe where physical laws construct the simplest constituents of matter into a vast cosmic web…Pain, misery and suffering are inextricably woven into the fabric of life. But they can be greatly minimized. Injustice can be done away with. Maybe it is now within our reach (in the next several hundred years or so) that we can create our own divine purpose and cooperatively build a better world. A moral world with fairness for all, without the need for religion. A world where each person has the right to diminished misery and suffering. A world where paradise is not just pie in the sky.

Note some of the assumptions embedded in this comment: 1) many injustices exist, 2) many of those injustices don't *have* to exist because humans have the ability to make things better, and 3) human lives matter.

On these three points, the Bible would agree.

We already saw in chapter 2 that human lives matter because every human is made in the image of God, and we saw in chapters 1 and 3 that God cares about the just functioning of societies (which, of course, assumes that injustices exist and that humans can do something about them). Consider a few additional verses from Scripture emphasizing how important justice is to God:

- Proverbs 31:8-9: "Open your mouth for the mute, for the rights of all who are destitute. Open your mouth, judge righteously, defend the rights of the poor and needy."

- Jeremiah 22:3: "Thus says the LORD: Do justice and righteousness, and deliver from the hand of the oppressor him who has been robbed. And do no wrong or violence to the resident alien, the fatherless, and the widow, nor shed innocent blood in this place."

- Micah: 6:8: "He has told you, O man, what is good; and what does the LORD require of you but to do justice, and to love kindness, and to walk humbly with your God?"

- Matthew 23:23: "Woe to you, scribes and Pharisees, hypocrites! For you tithe mint and dill and cumin, and have neglected the weightier matters of the law: justice and mercy and faithfulness. These you ought to have done, without neglecting the others."

Thus, the good news is that pretty much everyone agrees injustice exists and we can do something about it. Why, then, the hate from culture on this subject? Because we disagree on how to *define* injustice and what to *do* about it once we define it.

Defining Injustice

Recall from chapter 2 that justice is making right that which is wrong, and right and wrong are moral categories requiring a standard. To get us thinking about what that means again, imagine for a moment that you pour 1,000 puzzle pieces onto a table. You then take a wooden yardstick and lay it horizontally through the middle of the pieces, separating them into groups above and below the stick. You call the group above the stick the "right" pieces and the group below the stick the "wrong" pieces, with the location of the stick serving as the standard for determining which pieces are right and wrong. Believing that the "wrong" pieces below the stick need to be fixed in some way, you get to work righting the wrongs of the puzzle table.

But let's say someone doesn't like how you did things. They pick up the stick, mix all the pieces together, then place the stick in a different location to separate the pieces based on their own preferences. Now there are "right" and "wrong" groups again, but they're made up of different pieces than before because a different standard was used to separate them. This person, too, gets to work righting the wrongs of the puzzle table, but the pieces they're trying to fix are different than those the other person was trying to fix.

In this illustration, these two people would use similar vocabulary in saying that pieces are wrong and need to be made right, and they might even both be passionate about puzzle "justice." But because they used a different standard to determine which pieces were right or wrong in the first place, they were working to make *different wrongs right.*

This is why Christians and secular social justice activists have such divergent views on justice. As Christians, we know God's perfect character is the objective standard for determining what is right and wrong. He is the only accurate stick! Only His standards should be used to identify the wrongs that should be made right and to direct how we should work for biblically accurate notions of justice. *If you use any standards other than God's to define what's just or unjust, you're going to get justice wrong.* And that's precisely what's happening in culture today.

Injustice...According to Neo-Marxist Standards

What we've learned thus far is that Christians and secular social justice activists have different understandings of justice because we use different standards for defining the wrongs that should be made right. That's an important starting point for this discussion, but we need to go a step further now to explore the *nature* of the standard used by culture. This understanding will enable us to grasp why culture sees Christians not only as wrong but as power-hungry oppressors.

As I mentioned at the beginning of this chapter, secular social justice thinking is rooted in a philosophy called critical theory. Before recent years, relatively few people outside of certain academic and activist circles had heard of it. But after the organization Black Lives Matter (BLM) exploded into the public eye in 2020, the term *critical theory* (and especially the related concept of critical *race* theory) was suddenly propelled into popular-level discourse. BLM became a poster child for what critical theory–based social justice looks like in practice. But despite the fact that most people have now at least heard of critical theory, far fewer people have a clear understanding of its key concepts and their implications—in large part because it's a vast subject and it's easy to get lost in the details. My purpose here is not to do a deep dive into the minutiae, but rather, to highlight a few salient points that illustrate 1) how critical theory-based justice fundamentally differs from biblical notions of justice, and 2) how critical theory's framework leads to cultural outrage toward Christians.

To that end, let's start with a little history.

Critical theory is an academic discipline that grew out of Marxism. In the mid-1800s, Karl Marx argued that all of history had been one long economic class struggle between oppressed and oppressor groups. The oppressed, or proletariat, labored to produce goods, while the oppressors, or bourgeoisie, controlled the means of production.

Oppression, in this view, was the result of problematic social structures. As such, the only way the oppressed could be liberated was for them to gain a consciousness of their social location and overthrow the system in a revolution. The goal of these revolutionaries would be to create a new political order based on a socialist-defined notion of equality: equal outcome for all. Not equal *opportunity* for all—equal *outcome* for all.

Fast-forward to the 1930s. Intellectuals at the Frankfurt School in Germany took Marx's binary way of looking at the world through oppressor and oppressed categories and began extending it beyond economics. In the decades that followed, this framework was applied by various thinkers to race, gender, sexuality, and several other identity markers. Like the working class in Marx's analysis, people of color, women, and those in the LGBTQ community were identified as victims of social structures that kept them oppressed by those in power. They were considered oppressed because dominant groups were imposing their norms, values, and expectations on them.

The end result of this neo-Marxist analysis is a "social binary" in which everyone fits into one of two groups—oppressor or oppressed—based on each of their identity markers. Any given individual may fall into *both* oppressor and oppressed groups, depending on their unique mix of identity characteristics. For example, I am a white, heterosexual woman. That means I'm oppressed in terms of my gender, but I'm an oppressor in terms of my race and sexuality. Furthermore, people experience distinct forms of oppression based on their specific mix of memberships in oppressed groups (the interaction of these oppressions is called *intersectionality*). According to this view, a black trans woman experiences oppression at a different level and in a different way than someone like me, who is only oppressed in terms of gender but not race or sexuality.

It's important to understand that from the critical theory perspective, individuals don't have to experience anything in particular to be considered oppressed, nor do individuals have to do anything in particular to be considered oppressors. The oppressed-oppressor binary is a *social group phenomenon* based on presumed power dynamics in society. For example, in their book *Is Everyone Really Equal?*, critical theory scholars and advocates Özlem Sensoy and Robin DiAngelo write:

> To oppress is to hold down—to press—and deny a social group full access and potential in a given society. Oppression describes a set of policies, practices, traditions, norms, definitions, and explanations (discourses), which function to systematically exploit one social group to the benefit of another social group…Oppression occurs when one group is able to enforce its prejudice and discrimination throughout society because it controls the institutions. Oppression occurs at the group or macro level, and goes well beyond individuals. Sexism, racism, classism, ableism, and heterosexism are specific forms of oppression.[5]

From our discussion thus far, we can now identify the specific nature of the difference between biblical justice and critical theory–based justice: *In critical theory, the standard for identifying where the injustice of oppression lies is the dividing line of the social binary.* In other words, identity groups that hold the power in society (the oppressors) are, by definition, perpetrators of injustice, and identity groups with less power (the oppressed) are, by definition, victims of injustice. But, as we've already discussed, the only accurate standard for identifying justice and injustice is God's standard. God's standard isn't based on who does or doesn't hold power in society; it's based on His perfect moral character.

The result of this discrepancy in standards is that secular social justice advocates are often working to right injustices that aren't truly injustices because they've started with the false standard of a neo-Marxist social binary. And when Christians work for social outcomes in conflict with those deemed "just" according to critical theory, we're despised for our "oppressive" views.

It's helpful to see some tangible examples of how this plays out, so let's now look at two culturally high-profile branches of critical theory: critical race theory and queer theory.

Example 1: Critical Race Theory

Critical race theory (CRT) is the branch of critical theory that deals specifically with race-based oppression in society. According to CRT, white people are the oppressors and people of color are the oppressed; white people use their social privilege and power to impose *whiteness* on everyone else. Note that whiteness isn't about skin color, as the word might initially suggest. Rather, it's about the *culture* white people (problematically) impose on everyone else. The Smithsonian National Museum of African American History and Culture puts it this way:

> White dominant culture, or *whiteness*, refers to the ways white people and their traditions, attitudes and ways of life have been normalized over time and are now considered standard practices in the United States. And since white people still hold most of the institutional power in America, we have all internalized some aspects of white culture— including people of color.[6]

This definition comes from a graphic titled "Aspects and Assumptions of Whiteness in the United States." The graphic offers dozens of alleged examples of whiteness, including things like believing the nuclear family is the ideal social unit, rational thinking, the primacy of the Judeo-Christian tradition, Christianity being the norm, holidays based on "Christian religions," the belief that hard work is the key to success, respect for authority, being polite, and a preference for bland foods like steak and potatoes.

So much could be said about the examples on this list and on the chart more broadly, but for our current purpose, we'll stick with a single point. *Many examples of presumably problematic whiteness are not actually problematic.* Therein lies the issue. Critical theory starts from a belief that it's inherently unjust for a dominant group to impose its norms, values, and expectations on minority groups but never considers whether those norms, values, and expectations might be objectively good. It simply problematizes whatever is associated with the social group that holds the power. But what if, for example, God's ideal social unit *is* the nuclear family? That would make such a belief an accurate understanding of reality whether it's held by a dominant social group or not.

Contrary to critical theory's most basic assumptions, norms, values, and expectations are objectively good or bad regardless of who holds them. From a biblical perspective, racial injustice cannot be identified by the dividing line of CRT's social binary because no group is an oppressor or guilty of sin due solely to their skin color. People are guilty when they transgress God's moral law—full stop. It doesn't matter what their skin color is.

While this likely makes intuitive—as well as biblical—sense to most readers, it's a view that's disdained by those holding to CRT. Why? From the perspective of critical race theorists, Christians who reject CRT-based categories of justice aren't merely wrong in their views, they're complicit in turning a blind eye to what critical race proponents believe is evil racial oppression. You'll be met with grave moral indignation if you suggest that norms, values, and expectations can be evaluated on their own objective merits rather than as a function of group power dynamics. In fact, on the Smithsonian's graphic, objective thinking is listed as a trait of whiteness.

Furthermore, the resented concept of whiteness is closely associated with Christianity itself because America's predominantly white European heritage was also predominantly Christian. Ironically, this means that many (not all!) of the norms, values, and expectations associated with white people in America are objectively *good* because they originated from a Christian worldview...yet they're seen as *oppressive* because they happen to be associated with America's racially dominant group. For example, the nuclear family is part of God's objective design for human flourishing and has historically been an American norm given America's Christian heritage. However, CRT-based activists see the nuclear family as something to *abolish* because of its association with whiteness. Activists acknowledge this quite directly. As one put it, "There's no greater source of systematic oppression than the nuclear family. The nuclear family is associated with whiteness. And whiteness is associated with racism, bigotry, transphobia, and white supremacy."[7] If you search online for "Christianity and whiteness," you'll find numerous discussions of the supposed connection.[8]

Through the eyes of activists, then, Christians who reject CRT are guilty of upholding and defending racial injustice and are promoters of problematic "whiteness." But when we stand in the way of those working to tear down norms, values, and expectations that we know to be objectively good—for example, advocating for the common good by fighting for the protection of the nuclear family—we're actually doing what's right. And that's *true* justice.

Example 2: Queer Theory

Queer theory is the branch of critical theory that deals with gender identity and sexual oppression in society. According to queer theory, cisgender and heterosexual people are the oppressors and those in the LGBTQ community are the oppressed (cisgender refers to people whose gender identity corresponds with their biological sex). Whereas in CRT, oppressors impose *whiteness* on the oppressed, in queer theory, oppressors impose *cisheteronormativity* on the oppressed.

Cisheteronormativity refers to the idea that groups in power have arbitrarily made being cisgender and heterosexual the norms in society, thereby oppressing those who deviate from the norms. In other words, queer theorists claim that categories of gender (male and female) and sexuality (heterosexual and homosexual) are merely social constructs—ideas created by society rather than ideas reflecting any essential truth independent of society's beliefs. Anything heralded as a "normal" identity is therefore oppressive to those who have a different way of "being." To be queer, then, is to resist these normative power structures. As queer theorist David Halperin explains, "Queer is…whatever is at odds with the normal, the legitimate, the dominant. There is nothing in particular to which it necessarily refers. It is an identity without an essence."[9] Queer theory activists ultimately seek to rid society of its "oppressive" gender binary.

For those new to the subject, I realize this may sound like an obscure academic philosophy that could never leave the ivory tower. After all, it's quite hard for most of us to imagine a society that no longer acknowledges the existence of men and women in everyday life. But not only has this philosophy escaped the ivory tower, it's been adopted in K-12 schools nationwide. The public education system is just one of many places queer theory can be found, but it's an important one to know about given its influence on the next generation. Queer theory has infiltrated the educational system through supportive school district policies, formal teacher training, and gender and sexuality clubs established in more than 4,000 schools (we'll talk more about that in chapter 10).[10] The narrative is always the same: The gender binary has created an unjust society and we must now do the work of dismantling the cisheteronormativity that oppresses gender and sexual minorities. In practice, that can include anything from promoting a linguistic revolution (for example, calling men "people with a penis" and women "people with a vulva") to facilitating student gender transitions without parental consent, to encouraging boundless sexual experimentation…all in the name of justice.

But just as the false standard of the social binary incorrectly identifies racial oppression, the false standard of the social binary incorrectly identifies gender and sexual oppression. *It's not oppressive for society to have norms around gender and sexuality if those norms reflect God's design for humanity.* And Scripture is clear that both the gender binary and heterosexual marital unions are indeed God's design. Genesis 1:27 states, "God created man in his own image, in the image of God he created him; male and female he created them." Males and females are to come together in the unity of marriage and join as "one flesh" (Genesis 2:23-24; Matthew 19:3-6; Ephesians 5:28-32). And the Bible repeatedly condemns sexual behavior outside of marriage between a man and a woman (for example, Romans 1:26-27; 1 Corinthians 6:9-10; 7:2-5; Hebrews 13:4). Just as we saw with CRT, what's normal or socially dominant isn't necessarily bad. It might or might not be. In the case of gender and sexuality, however, the norms against which secular social justice activists rail are part of God's objectively good design.

Once again, we find that in the eyes of culture, Christians are guilty of upholding oppressive norms that perpetuate injustice and harm. But if we work to tear down gender and sexuality norms in the name of justice, we're actually working against what God Himself wants for humanity. Our love for God and our love for others should lead us to actively work *against* queer theory's manifestations in culture because falsehoods about gender and sexuality are what truly cause harm.

Christianity Is Life-Giving, Not Oppressive

Given our preceding discussion, we can now apply our understanding to Pavlovitz's comments from the beginning of this chapter and answer some of the questions raised. It makes for a helpful case study.

Why did Pavlovitz think it was relevant to repeatedly point out that the people who wrote the Dallas Statement were white men? Because he presumes—in accordance with critical theory—that the views held by dominant social groups (in this case, white men) are inherently oppressive.

Why did he suggest the writers wanted a Christianity that secured their privilege and hoarded their power? Because he presumes—in accordance with critical theory—that claims of objective truth are a disguised power play by dominant social groups who want to retain their privilege.

Why did he claim that biblical views on race, gender, and sexuality "resist equality, curb diversity, and keep marginalized people where they are"? Because he presumes—in accordance with critical theory—that if you define, defend, and seek justice in terms other than those corresponding with the standard of the social binary, your motivations are to keep marginalized social groups down. In doing so, you allegedly demonstrate that you don't want all groups to be equal and you don't value diversity because you want to keep benefitting from your dominant group's social privilege.

Yes, you practically need a specialized dictionary to translate critical theory thinking.

Understanding the linguistic equivocation involved, however, is half the battle. When culture wrongly charges us with perpetuating oppression, injustice, and harm, it's initially tempting to be shamed into silence. No one likes being on the receiving end of such alarming accusations. But there's a certain amount of resiliency the body of Christ must gain in the face of today's moral condemnation. We have to remember that words like these are lobbed based on a false standard. When we work to make right that which is wrong in society as defined by God's standards—and work *against* evil perpetrated in the name of justice as defined by culture's standards—we embody life-giving truth for the common good. And truth is *never* oppressive. It's what sets people free.

QUICK RESPONSES TO 5 POPULAR CHALLENGES
on Social Justice

1. Jesus was a social justice warrior. Christians should be too.[11]

(Questions: How do you define social justice? What do you mean by social justice warrior? What are some examples in Scripture that you think demonstrate how Jesus saw social justice in the same sense as you do?)

Jesus certainly cared about justice, but He didn't define justice in the same way as many social justice advocates do today. In today's culture, injustice is defined in terms of the power dynamics between entire social groups (for example, men versus women, white people versus people of color, and so on). But the Bible defines justice based on God's objective standards of right and wrong *regardless* of who holds power in society, so Jesus's view of justice is often at odds with the view typically held by those labeled *social justice warriors* today.

2. Critical theory is just an analytical tool, so Christians opposing it are overreacting.

(Questions: Can you explain what you mean by "just an analytical tool"? Are you saying that those who adhere to critical theory don't seek action based on critical theory's analysis? Do you believe analytical tools are inherently neutral, or is it possible that some tools can lead to the wrong social diagnosis and solution?)

There are significant problems with critical theory from a biblical perspective *even as* an analytical tool, but it's not accurate to say that those who embrace critical theory merely want everyone to analyze the world in the same way. They do want that, but they also want to use that analysis to revolutionize the structure of society to achieve ends that are at odds with a biblical understanding of justice.

Critical theory's analysis of society fundamentally differs with that of the Bible because it bases its definition of oppression on the social binary rather than on God's objective standards of right and wrong.

3. Christianity is oppressive to the LGBTQ community.

(Questions: What do you mean by oppressive? Do you think Christians are oppressive, biblical teachings are oppressive, or both? Can you share some examples of oppressive Christianity?)

The Bible teaches that every human is equally and inherently valuable and that Christians are to love everyone accordingly—the LGBTQ community and everyone else. The Bible *also* teaches that God has a design for human gender and sexuality, and when we don't live in accordance with that design, we sin against God and harm ourselves. It's not oppressive to disagree with someone else's views on morality; if it were, that would mean the LGBTQ community is oppressive to Christians as well.

4. Christians who reject CRT ignore systemic racial oppression.

(Questions: What kinds of modern systemic oppression do you have in mind? How do you define CRT? Do you think it's possible to believe examples of systemic racial oppression exist without accepting CRT as the lens through which we should identify and end them?)

Christians who reject CRT do believe that systemic racial oppression can be a reality and has been a reality (slavery is an obvious example). However, CRT prescribes a specific way of evaluating systemic racism through the lens of the social binary. Christians who reject CRT are rejecting CRT's method of defining, identifying, and ending systemic racism, *not* rejecting that systemic racism can exist or that Christians should work to abolish such racism when accurately identified according to God's standards.

5. Christianity is a white man's religion (and is therefore oppressive).

(Questions: What do you mean by "white man's religion"? Do you believe that religions can be true or false? If so, do you believe that the truthfulness or falsehood of any given religion can be determined by its association with any particular group of people? Why or why not?)

There's no doubt that throughout history people have committed all kinds of atrocities in the name of Christianity, and many people associate Christianity with white slaveholders or violent white European colonizers. However, whether it's with respect to this subject or any other, we have to recognize that there can be a serious divergence between the actions of people who claim the name of Christ and what the Bible actually teaches. The truthfulness of Christianity doesn't stand or fall on how people (of any race) have used or misused biblical teachings; it stands or falls on whether or not Jesus was raised from the dead (1 Corinthians 15:14).

ACTIONS FOR THE COMMON GOOD:
7 Ways to Shine Your Light Through Biblical Justice

As an overarching note about several of the following ideas, always check with organizations to see if they receive government funding. If they do, they're likely to be subject to rules that enforce adherence to critical theory–based principles (for example, human resources training that promotes acceptance of CRT and queer theory among employees, company-wide affirmation and enforcement of desired transgender pronouns, approaches to helping people that are at odds with biblical notions of justice, and so on). That's not to say Christian organizations that do *not* accept government funding are always biblical in their approach to justice, nor is it to say that Christian organizations which *do* accept government funding are always unbiblical. Funding, however, is one significant factor to consider. Christians should thoroughly vet *any* organization they choose to support.

1. **Pray for, volunteer with, or donate to Christian organizations dedicated to poverty and disaster relief around the world.** There are many such organizations, and they have differing approaches, focal points, and financial structures. Start with an online search for "Christian poverty relief organizations" and take the time to educate yourself well on any given organization's faith commitment and approach before offering support. Even popular charity evaluation websites have their own biases, so it's important to do your own analysis.

2. **Pray for, volunteer with, or donate to Christian organizations dedicated to eliminating human trafficking and rehabilitating survivors.** Human trafficking is the exploitation of men, women, and children in order to gain a profit—a modern form of slavery. An estimated 27.6 million

trafficking victims worldwide are forced or compelled to work in a variety of abusive settings such as brothels and factories.[12] Search online for "Christian organizations fighting human trafficking" to learn more about work you can get involved with. Some of these organizations focus on international needs, while others may work in your local area (yes, there's a significant amount of human trafficking that happens in the United States).

3. **Pray for, volunteer with, or donate to Christian organizations fighting religious persecution.** It's estimated that 365 million Christians suffer high levels of persecution and discrimination for their faith.[13] There are a number of Christian organizations that exist to combat this persecution worldwide. Search online for "Christian organizations fighting religious persecution," and, again, take the time to educate yourself well on any given organization's work and approach before offering support.

4. **Pray for, volunteer with, or donate to gospel rescue missions.** Gospel rescue missions are transitional living facilities that provide those living in destitute conditions (for example, the hungry, homeless, abused, or addicted) with opportunities for life transformation through education, training, counseling, and discipleship. There are more than 300 such organizations across the US. Find the one closest to you at www.citygatenetwork.org. Note that gospel rescue missions within this network function independently and differ in their programs and funding sources. Vet your local gospel rescue mission accordingly.

5. **Provide a home to children temporarily or permanently separated from their birth family.** More than 600,000

children pass through the foster care system in the US each year, with more than 100,000 waiting to be adopted.[14] Christians can provide much-needed stability for foster children or a permanent family for those waiting for adoption. Requirements vary by state; search online for "how to foster in (fill in your state)" or "how to adopt in (fill in your state)." For those who want to help children in crisis on a shorter-term basis, the Safe Families for Children program works with churches to match children with hosts—often for mere hours or weeks at a time.[15] And even if you don't get involved directly with one of these programs, work with your church to support those who do! You can provide babysitting relief, financial assistance, clothing or toy donations, and more to families supporting kids in these ways.

6. **Help make it possible for low-income and single-parent families in your church community to choose homeschooling or Christian private schools.** More and more Christian parents are looking for alternatives to public education, but the reality is that these choices can be out of reach for many families. Consider ways your church can pool financial and logistical resources to provide educational choices for kids who might otherwise not have those opportunities.

7. **Find out more about and get involved in your church's service opportunities.** There are all kinds of outreach possibilities that aren't reflected here—this is just a small sampling of ideas. Your local church is likely already partnering with certain ministries or running its own ministries that you can get involved in. Talk to your church leadership to find out what you can do.

CHAPTER 8

CONTROLLING MISOGYNISTS

The View from Pro-Choice Activists

■ ■ ■

On June 24, 2022, the US Supreme Court issued its history-making decision in the case of *Dobbs v. Jackson Women's Health Organization*: There is no constitutional right to abortion.

The 6-3 decision overturned the 1973 Supreme Court ruling in the case of *Roe v. Wade*, which had declared that a state law banning abortions except to save the life of the mother was unconstitutional. *Roe v. Wade* resulted in a federal right to abortion...and the subsequent killing of more than 63 million babies.[1]

Pro-life Christians immediately celebrated the *Dobbs* decision as an incredible win, but the response from the pro-choice culture was one of outrage, indignation, and dismay: *How could the Supreme Court take away women's rights?*

Some of that response started with the dissenting justices on the case. Justices Stephen Breyer, Sonia Sotomayor, and Elena Kagan said the Court's decision meant that "after today, young women will come of age with fewer rights than their mothers and grandmothers had."[2] They gravely warned that "from the very moment of fertilization, a woman has no rights to speak of. A state can force her to bring a pregnancy to term even at the steepest personal and familial costs."[3]

The narrative that women were being stripped of basic reproductive rights, effectively putting their bodies under the control of a government forcing them to give birth, was an emotionally powerful motivator for the pro-choice cause. Activists seized on the opportunity to label those who are pro-life *forced birthers*, drew continual parallels to the dystopian novel *The Handmaid's Tale* (in which a theocratic government forces subservient women to bear children), rallied and protested across the country, and turned social media into a platform for rage.

It also wasn't lost on the pro-choice culture that the pro-life movement is closely associated with Christianity or so-called religion more broadly, and indignation was directed accordingly. A *New York Times* writer claimed, for example:

> It was not constitutional analysis but religious doctrine that drove the opposition to Roe. And it was the court's unacknowledged embrace of religious doctrine that has turned American women into desperate refugees fleeing their home states in pursuit of reproductive health care that less than a month ago was theirs by right.[4]

A variety of media outlets additionally tried to convince Christians they don't *have* to be pro-life—that's just the view of religious *extremists*. A *Rolling Stone* headline, for example, read: "Think Christianity Is Anti-Abortion? Think Again. Extremists have sought to use religion as a tool to dominate women's bodies, but Christians have a long history of being in favor of abortion rights."[5]

Culture's message was quite clear after the *Dobbs* decision: Women had lost important rights and religious people (typically Christians) were to blame. But the summer of 2022, of course, wasn't the end of the story. It was just the beginning of a new story because *Dobbs* didn't make abortion illegal, it only gave abortion policy decisions back to individual states. Across America, states are now engaged in heated internal battles over the fate of millions of babies, and those battles will last well into the future.

It's hard to imagine an issue where more is at stake for the common good than policies allowing for the murder of babies at will. And if the word *murder* seems unnecessarily harsh or shocking, that's a symptom in and of itself of how culture has successfully trained us to view abortion in sugarcoated terms. As Christians, we can't afford to not see clearly. Millions of lives hang in the balance.

In this chapter, we're going to cut through culture's confusion to see abortion for what it is and gain the clarity needed to advocate for righteousness in the midst of today's greatest evil.

Understanding the Lost Rights of the *Dobbs* Decision

Because so much of the cultural narrative on abortion revolves around the language of rights—especially in the aftermath of *Dobbs*—we need to start by establishing an understanding of which rights were lost, why they were lost, and if the loss of rights is inherently a bad thing.

When *Roe v. Wade* was passed in 1973, the Supreme Court had concluded that a right of privacy was inherent in the Due Process Clause of the Fourteenth Amendment. The justices furthermore inferred that privacy included "a woman's decision whether or not to terminate her pregnancy."[6] However, the original purpose of the Fourteenth Amendment, ratified in 1868, was far removed from granting abortion rights. Its purpose was to grant citizenship to all persons born or naturalized in the United States—including formerly enslaved persons—and provide all citizens equal protection of the law. More specifically, it says this:

> No State shall make or enforce any law which shall abridge
> the privileges or immunities of citizens of the United States;

nor shall any State deprive any person of life, liberty, or property, without due process of law; nor deny to any person within its jurisdiction the equal protection of the laws.[7]

Though the Court's majority opinion, written by Justice Harry Blackmun, acknowledged that the Constitution does not *explicitly* mention any right of privacy, the justices stated that there was an *implied* right to privacy and then inferred that privacy would include a woman's right to "terminate" her pregnancy. Just like that, a constitutional right to abortion was found.

If that sounds like a big legal stretch, you're on your way to understanding why the Supreme Court eventually reversed the decision in 2022.

Writing for the Court majority in *Dobbs*, Justice Samuel Alito said that the ruling in *Roe* was "egregiously wrong" and its reasoning "exceptionally weak"—going so far as to call *Roe* an "abuse of judicial authority."[8] Justice Alito wrote that the only legitimate unenumerated rights (rights not explicitly stated in the Constitution) are those "deeply rooted in the Nation's history and tradition" and "implicit in the concept of ordered liberty."[9] The majority on the Court held that abortion is not such a right and concluded, "The authority to regulate abortion must be returned to the people and their elected representatives."[10]

That last line is especially important. The justices in *Dobbs* weren't making a statement about the morality of abortion, they weren't making abortion illegal, and they weren't trying to reflect popular opinion on the subject (three common misconceptions). *They were concluding that a judicial error had been made in* Roe *because the Court at the time had asserted a constitutional right that didn't exist.* And if there's no constitutional right to abortion, then abortion policies going forward would necessarily fall under the jurisdiction of individual states.

We now have answers to the questions of which rights were lost and why they were lost: A constitutional right to abortion was "lost" because it had been given in error in the first place. If all 50 states now want to give women unfettered rights to kill their preborn babies, they can still do so. The Court simply concluded that the Constitution itself doesn't confer that right.

That leads to our final question on rights: Is the loss of rights inherently a bad thing? For many people, the answer seems to be a foregone conclusion of yes. Recall, for example, that the dissenting justices themselves wrote, "After today, young women will come of age with fewer rights than their mothers and grandmothers had." The embedded assumption is that fewer rights relative to an earlier time is inherently problematic. But that isn't necessarily the case. To see why, we need to understand the difference between God-given and government-given rights.

God-given rights are those that precede any human law; they're rights that every human being is entitled to by virtue of their humanity. The Founding Fathers in America referenced such rights in the Declaration of Independence: "We hold these truths to be self-evident, that all men are created equal, that they are endowed by their Creator with certain unalienable Rights, that among these are Life, Liberty and the pursuit of Happiness."[11] The US Constitution was designed to protect those rights from government violation. Importantly, God-given rights are, by definition, objectively good because they're rooted in the authority and nature of a perfect God. The loss of a God-given right, therefore, *is* inherently bad—a person is losing something good to which they're entitled by their Creator.

Government-given rights, on the other hand, can be arbitrarily given and taken away at the discretion of those in power because these rights aren't rooted in an authority higher than the state. That also means government-given rights are not necessarily good. As an obvious example, Americans had the government-given right to hold slaves. The government later took away that right. Virtually no one today laments the loss of slaveholding rights because we recognize that it was a right people *shouldn't have had in the first place*. In fact, *Dobbs* was one of several cases in history where the Supreme Court reversed its own rulings. In 1896, for example, in *Plessy v. Ferguson*, the Court affirmed the right of states to maintain racially segregated public facilities, in a doctrine of "separate but equal." But in 1954, the Court reversed the ruling in *Brown v. Board of Education*, stating that separate educational facilities are inherently unequal. Whether the loss of a government-given right is good or bad therefore depends on whether the right itself is good or bad. If it's a right to do evil— for example, to enslave another human as property—then the loss of that right is actually a good thing.

So, when people are outraged or indignant over the idea that women "lost rights," we need to remember that losing government-given rights isn't necessarily bad. The language has a strong emotional pull, but as Christians, we need to think more deeply: Is the government-given right to kill a preborn baby an objectively good right we should want to protect? Or is it an objectively bad right that we should want to abolish?

To answer those questions, we need clarity on the morality of abortion.

Abortion Isn't Complicated

While Christians are the religious group most often associated with the pro-life movement, research shows that 33 percent of evangelical Protestants, 52 percent of Historically Black Protestants, and 60 percent of mainline Protestants believe abortion should be legal in all or most cases.[12] Clearly, even many Christians consider themselves pro-choice and joined culture in lamenting the *Dobbs* decision. A woman on Reddit shared, for example:

> I broke down crying during church today, and I don't
> know if I have any faith left in this country, or people in

general. I'm just disappointed, furious and depressed. My pastor decided to talk briefly on stage about Roe v. Wade outcome. He is pro-life and believes this is such wonderful news to hear. I hear a few other men in the chapel raise their voice saying, "Amen," in approval. Women are having their rights taken away from them and people cheer. I don't ever plan on having children, and I am just upset. It feels like I have just lost my love for God, and others here at church and I need to step away from the church for now.[13]

Many Christians believe abortion is such a complicated issue that we should agree to disagree in order to not drive women like this one away from the church.

But the morality of abortion isn't complicated at all.

The *circumstances* that lead to unwanted pregnancies may be complicated, but those circumstances don't change the *morality* of ending a life; abortion is emotionally complicated but not morally so. Note that separating a person's circumstances from the morality of their actions isn't unique to the abortion conversation. No one makes the case, for example, that we need to allow people to rape others because difficult life circumstances can result in a person feeling the desire or need to sexually assault someone else. Societies determine that rape is wrong and make it illegal accordingly—no matter what kind of awful life circumstances a perpetrator may have had that contributed to their actions.

The question we need to answer and focus on, then, is this: Is it morally wrong to intentionally kill a preborn human being? And we can readily answer that question with just two points.

First, the Bible unequivocally condemns the intentional taking of innocent human life. Perhaps most obviously, the sixth commandment states, "You shall not murder" (Exodus 20:13). As some other examples, Genesis 9:6 says, "Whoever sheds the blood of man, by man shall his blood be shed, for God made man in his own image." God says in Exodus 23:7, "Keep far from a false charge, and do not kill the innocent and righteous, for I will not acquit the wicked." And Proverbs 6:16-17 says, "There are six things that the LORD hates, seven that are an abomination to him: haughty eyes, a lying tongue, and hands that shed innocent blood..." (see also Leviticus 24:17; Matthew 5:21-22; 1 John 3:12; Revelation 21:8).

Second, we know from both the Bible and science that preborn babies are, indeed, human. Although the Bible doesn't explicitly state that the preborn are human, it speaks in ways that assume as much. Consider, for example, the following verses:[14]

- God said to the prophet Jeremiah: "Before I formed you in the womb I knew you, and before you were born I consecrated you; I appointed you a prophet to the nations" (Jeremiah 1:5).

- "You formed my inward parts; you knitted me together in my mother's womb" (Psalm 139:13).

- "The LORD called me from the womb, from the body of my mother he named my name" (Isaiah 49:1).

- "He will be filled with the Holy Spirit, even from his mother's womb" (Luke 1:15).

- "When Elizabeth heard the greeting of Mary, the baby leaped in her womb. And Elizabeth was filled with the Holy Spirit" (Luke 1:41).

Furthermore, the science of embryology affirms that human embryos are not creatures of a different kind from human beings, but rather, are human beings at a different stage of development. One leading embryology textbook, for example, describes embryos this way: "Human development beings at fertilization when a sperm fuses with an oocyte to form a single cell, the zygote. This highly specialized, totipotent cell (capable of giving rise to any cell type) marks the beginning of each of us as a unique individual."[15] Thus, the moment sperm and egg come together, a unique human being is formed.

Pro-choice activists sometimes try to avoid the implications of this undeniable fact by making a distinction between a human and a "person." They claim that there are certain criteria a human must meet to have the value we normally associate with humanity (thereby qualifying them as a "person" with the right to life). The Bible, of course, makes no such distinction in value between humans. But even those who don't look to the Bible as their authority for truth normally recognize that differences in human characteristics don't determine whether we should be able to kill someone or not. They just don't apply the same logic if it happens to be a *preborn* human.

Consider, for example, Stephen D. Schwarz's helpful SLED acronym, which highlights how four key differences between embryos and adults are nonessential: ṣize, ḷevel of development, ẹnvironment, and ḍegree of dependency.[16] In each of these categories, a difference also exists between *toddlers* and adults, but virtually no one suggests we should justify the killing of *toddlers* based on these differences. For example:

- **Size:** Humans are smaller as embryos, but when else do we use body size to determine value? Virtually no one suggests we should be able to kill a toddler just because they're smaller than a six-foot-tall adult.

- **Level of Development:** Embryos are less developed than adults, but toddlers are also less developed than adults. People don't normally argue that there's a sliding scale of human value as we develop mentally and physically throughout childhood.

- **Environment:** We don't accept the killing of toddlers based on where they're located, so why would we accept the killing of embryos based on where they're located? Or, as pro-life speaker and author Scott Klusendorf asks, "How does a journey of 8 inches down the birth canal change the essential nature of the [preborn] from a being we can kill to one we can't?"[17]

- **Degree of Dependency:** Embryos depend on their mothers for survival, but so do toddlers. Dependence on another human doesn't determine when it's acceptable to kill someone—if it did, we should be free to kill toddlers as well.

In short, preborn babies are human beings and there's no logically consistent reason to assign a lesser value to their lives based on differences like these.

We can now summarize the pro-life rationale in the form of a simple syllogism (drawing a conclusion from two stated premises):

1. It's morally wrong to intentionally kill an innocent human being. *We learned this from the Bible.*[18]

2. Abortion intentionally kills an innocent human being. *We learned this from the Bible and science.*

3. Therefore, abortion is morally wrong. *This conclusion necessarily follows from the preceding two premises.*

As we can see from this brief section, the morality of abortion isn't complicated; it's quite clear. Abortion is the intentional taking of innocent human life. It's murder. And, again, more than 63 million babies have been aborted since 1973. Christians should recognize abortion as one of the greatest acts of evil against individual humans and the common good today—a government-given right we should unequivocally seek to eliminate.[19]

Beyond Lost Rights: Breaking Down the Charges

If 1) abortion is murder and 2) nearly everyone agrees that murder is morally wrong, how is it that culture is overwhelmingly in favor of having the choice to abort? And not just in favor of having the choice, but enraged at those who are opposed to it?

If we really stop to think about this, these questions should be baffling. Unless people are making the case that murder isn't *ever* morally wrong (a position that exists but is rare), it would be logically consistent to conclude culture would be against the killing of preborn babies as much as it's against the killing of anyone else. But, of course, that's not what we see.

For some, the answer to why that's the case is that they're "just okay" with the murder of certain categories of humans and don't feel the need to offer further justification for their pro-choice position. Television host Bill Maher, for example, said this:

> I can respect the absolutist position. I really can. I scold the left on when they say, "Oh, you know what, they just hate women, people who aren't...pro-choice." They don't hate women. They just made that up. They think it's murder. And it kind of is. I'm just okay with that. I am. I mean, there's eight billion people in the world. I'm sorry, we won't miss you. That's my position on that.[20]

Maher's statement is chilling yet honest. Few people are willing to be so blunt about their willingness to just be "okay" with some forms of murder. But don't let the chill factor distract you from the important insight that otherwise underlies Maher's words: *Pro-choice advocates primarily frame the debate from the perspective of the woman, whereas pro-life advocates primarily frame it from the perspective of the preborn baby.* More specifically, pro-choice advocates focus on the (alleged) harm to women that comes from *not* having the right to abort, whereas pro-life advocates focus on the harm to preborn babies that comes from women *having* the right to abort.

Therein lies the answer to our earlier questions. Culture is overwhelmingly pro-choice despite believing murder is wrong because it typically isn't even thinking about abortion as an issue of harm to preborn babies—it's thinking of it as an issue of harm to women. And that distinction is also the source of the emotional outrage on the subject. Culture doesn't only see Christians and other pro-life advocates as wrong; it sees them as *misogynistic oppressors*.

Furthermore, this explains why there's often so much confusion on the topic, even amongst Christians. When the central question of whether it's morally wrong to intentionally kill a preborn human being is clouded by claims of harm done to women, people start losing conviction that the morality of abortion is dictated by what happens to the baby. They start to believe that the (alleged) harm done to women in taking away their right to abortion is equal to or greater than the harm done to a baby in taking away their life.

As we've already discussed, Christians should understand with incisive clarity that it's morally wrong to intentionally kill a preborn baby. But are there also moral wrongs being committed against women when we protect those babies' lives? Are pro-life advocates looking at only half of the necessary picture? Let's evaluate four of the most popular claims of harm to women in order to answer these questions.

Claim 1: Pro-life advocates want to control women's bodies ("my body, my choice").

Any time you advocate for a position on *any* subject and a person responds with something to the effect of "You just want to…," it's important to recognize that they're questioning your *motivation* for the position, and that's a separate question from the *rightness* of your position. In this example, if it's morally wrong to intentionally kill a preborn human being, then it's morally wrong regardless of why any given person holds that position.

That said, the central claim here is that pro-life advocates are harming women by oppressively trying to control their bodies. This claim, however, fails on logic alone. Our society has laws against murder because we've collectively agreed that it's wrong to intentionally kill an innocent human being. It's no more controlling, therefore, to have restrictions on what would-be murderers do with their bodies to kill others than it is to have restrictions on what pregnant women do with *their* bodies to kill others (and, again, we know scientifically that preborn babies are indeed "others"—unique humans with their own set of DNA). If it's morally wrong to intentionally kill a preborn human being, it's not harmful to have laws "controlling" whether women can use their bodies to do so.

Claim 2: Pro-life policies impose trauma on women and kids because kids are being forced into the world in bad circumstances.

A popular meme shared on social media after the *Dobbs* decision is representative of this kind of thinking: "Ending abortion will bring nothing but pain. Not only for women, but for children. Children will be born to parents who can't afford them, parents who aren't ready, or they will live their lives in foster care. More poor kids, more abused kids, more traumatized kids."

Consider the logic as it applies to both women and kids.

First, does it harm women if they're unable to kill a preborn baby and consequently have to raise that child in less-than-desirable circumstances? A mom certainly may struggle emotionally, physically, or financially, and raising the child may even require her to take a vastly different path in life than the one she would have. *But that's true even for moms who give birth to babies they want.* Moms can cherish their kids *and* struggle to raise them. The circumstances themselves, then, aren't harmful—the difficulty of some circumstances is simply *unwelcome* by moms who have an undesired pregnancy. And the degree to which a mom happens to be willing to endure difficult circumstances to raise her child has no bearing on whether it's wrong to intentionally kill that child before they're born. Future hardship doesn't justify murder.

But what about the child? What if the mom is going to abuse the child if she can't kill him or her?

Let me ask you this: Would we ever pose that question if the child in question were a toddler? Of course not! Any mom could justify killing her child by saying the child was better off dead given the abuse she would have put them through. Is there a worse form of abuse than murder? If we recognize the threat of abuse is not a justification for killing a toddler, we should recognize it's also not a justification for killing a preborn baby.

And finally, it's worth noting that no woman is forced to raise a child just because she can't have an abortion. Adoption placement is a wonderful option for many.

Claim 3: Pro-life policies force a woman to bear her rapist's child.

One of the concerns raised by the dissenting justices in the *Dobbs* decision was that some states would go so far as to have no exceptions for rape or incest: "Under those laws, a woman will have to bear her rapist's child or a young girl her father's—no matter if doing so will destroy her life."[21] The assumption, of course, is that everyone knows there *should* be exceptions in these cases.

This is probably the challenge that pro-life Christians struggle with the most, because rape and incest are undoubtedly horrific. Many people instinctively want to minimize the suffering of rape and incest victims by not requiring them to give birth (which seems like a further trauma). But two wrongs don't make a right.

In these cases, the woman is a victim of violence—a tragic moral wrong. If she has an abortion, then the preborn baby is an *additional* victim of violence—another tragic moral wrong. Let's be clear: The harm done to a woman in these cases is by the rapist, not by laws restricting abortion. The only just response to rape and incest is to punish the criminal, not the innocent preborn baby. Many pro-life ministries offer counseling to women who are victims of rape or incest and can help with the placement of a child for adoption if desired.

Claim 4: Pro-life policies cause women to die because they can't get lifesaving abortion care.

In extremely rare cases, pregnancy threatens a woman's life. For example, in a tubal ectopic pregnancy, the embryo implants on the wall of a fallopian tube rather than on the wall of the uterus. The fallopian tube is too narrow for a baby to continue developing, so if no action is taken, the tube can burst and cause an internal hemorrhage that's fatal to the mom. There's currently no way to transfer the embryo to a place where it can continue developing, so in order to save the mom's life, doctors have to end the embryo's life through surgical removal or medication. *There is not a single state law that prevents a physician from treating an ectopic pregnancy to save the mom's life—including in states that restrict abortion.* In fact, the Charlotte Lozier Institute has extensively documented state-by-state abortion laws to show that *every* state with abortion restrictions permits abortion in circumstances when necessary to save the mother's life (whether due to an ectopic pregnancy or other medical condition).[22] Additionally, states universally recognize the distinction between miscarriage and abortion and never limit the treatment of miscarriage despite popular claims to the contrary (miscarriage is the spontaneous and naturally occurring death of a developing baby, whereas abortion is the intentional killing of the developing baby).

Simply put, the claim that a woman will be left to die if a pregnancy threatens her life is a myth.

That said, readers may wonder how ending a preborn baby's life is morally justified in saving the mother's life if we're going to maintain consistency with the stand that it's morally wrong to intentionally kill a preborn human being at any other time. But these circumstances are not morally equivalent. Dr. Christina Francis, a board-certified OB/GYN and CEO of the American Association of Pro-Life Obstetricians and Gynecologists, explains the reasoning well:

> The sole intent of an abortion is to produce a dead baby—that's why it's called a "failed abortion" when the baby survives. Treating a pregnancy complication that threatens the mother's life to save her life, such as ectopic pregnancy, does not intend to cause the death of the preborn child. Our treatment intends to save the life of the mother. As pro-life physicians, we are pro-life for both mother and baby, so the decision is clear—we save who we can.[23]

Bringing Moral Clarity to Light

From culture's perspective, the *Dobbs* decision was a catastrophic assault on women. The Supreme Court had stripped women of their basic reproductive rights and set them back decades in progress toward gender equality. They would be forced to give birth by a government that controlled what they could and couldn't do with their own bodies. They would be crushed under the burdens of raising a child they never wanted. They would be forced to bear their rapist's child. They would die from not being able to access lifesaving care when pregnancies threatened their lives. Women were being oppressed, and that was a matter worthy of the gravest moral outrage.

It all sounds quite dire…if you don't have the clarity that abortion is murder and that the claims above are morally, logically, or factually confused, as we've seen in this chapter.

If Christians won't bring this clarity to light, who will? Do we care more about agreeing to disagree than about the wholesale slaughter of hundreds of thousands of babies each year? Lord, let it not be. May we never be more blinded by culture's darkness than we're alert to the need to expose it.

QUICK RESPONSES TO 5 POPULAR CHALLENGES
on Abortion

We already covered several challenges in the course of this chapter, especially as they relate to how abortion allegedly harms women. The challenges that follow are popular claims that don't directly correspond with the points covered in this chapter but are still important for Christians to understand in the abortion debate.

1. Pro-choice doesn't mean pro-abortion. I don't love abortion, but women should have the right to choose.

(Questions: Why don't you love abortion? What about it do you think is undesirable or wrong? Do you believe it's morally wrong to intentionally kill a preborn human being? If so, why do you believe people should have the option to do so? What do you believe are negative consequences that would come from not giving women the choice to abort?)

Imagine for a moment that I were someone who thought slavery was morally wrong but still claimed to be pro-choice on the matter—a "pro-choice doesn't mean proslavery" position. I'm guessing you would find that position detestable because nearly everyone today recognizes that slavery was an evil institution in our society; it's not a matter we believe people should *ever* be able to make choices about based on their own preferences. In the same way, abortion is the intentional killing of a preborn baby—murder—and that, too, is a matter on which no one should be able to choose.

2. Pro-life laws are racist because rich white women will still be able to get abortions even if abortion is outlawed.

(Questions: Do you believe it's racist if people of all races don't have the same opportunity to murder? Why or why not?)

Your comment presupposes that the ability to have an abortion is a *good* thing, so if not everyone has access to it, that's a *bad* thing. But those who are pro-life believe that it's morally wrong to intentionally kill a preborn human being—that it's murder—and it should therefore be against the law just as the murder of any other human is. And if abortion is indeed murder, then it's not racist to have laws against it even *if* certain groups are better able to skirt the law than others; societies should work to provide equal opportunity for good, not bad.

3. Pro-life advocates are hypocrites who don't care about the lives of babies after they're born.

(Questions: What would it look like from your perspective to demonstrate care for babies after they're born? If a person doesn't do those things, how does that make them hypocritical with respect to their position on the morality of abortion itself? How did you come to the conclusion that pro-life advocates don't care about babies after they're born?)

Pro-life advocates are opposed to abortion because they believe that it's morally wrong to intentionally kill a preborn human being. Whether a given person who holds a pro-life position does or does not do any particular thing for babies after they're born has no bearing on whether the position itself is morally correct (consider, for example, that if a person opposed to rape does nothing for rape victims, we still know that their opposition to rape is the morally correct position to hold, and we don't call them hypocrites). That said, Christians do love and care about all people, and many Christian ministries exist to provide support to families in need.

4. You should keep your religion out of my uterus.

(Questions: What do you mean by religion? Do you believe society should ever allow laws that are based on values held by religious people, or do you believe we should only allow laws based on values held by atheists? If you believe it's okay to pass laws that incorporate values held by religious people, where do you draw the line on which ones should not be allowed?)

As a society, we make laws all the time that are based on values held by religious people—for example, we outlaw murder, and murder is considered morally wrong by nearly every religious group. We're not legislating anyone's personal religion when we pass laws against something like murder; we're legislating a moral position. In a democracy, everyone is welcome to bring their moral views to bear on how they vote regardless of whether those views are religiously motivated or not.

5. Men have no right to tell a woman what she can or can't do with her body.

(Questions: How did you come to that conclusion? Do you believe that principle applies to issues other than abortion? For example, do you believe men should have a say in whether women can use their bodies to drink and drive? Why or why not?)

In a democracy, both men and women vote on what they believe is best for society, including what both men and women can do with their bodies (for example, we don't allow men or women to use their bodies to drink and drive). In the case of abortion, pro-life advocates believe it's morally wrong to kill a preborn human being just as it's morally wrong to kill any other human being. The gender of a person holding a position has no bearing on the morality of the action itself.

ACTIONS FOR THE COMMON GOOD:
7 Ways to Shine Your Light Through Pro-Life Advocacy

1. **Stay informed about abortion-related bills in your state and take action accordingly.** Action, of course, includes voting against any bill supporting the destruction of life, but there's more you can do! Help bring awareness about pending legislation to your church and everyone you know. Many Christians don't stay up to date on legislation, even on issues as important as abortion, so you can help make an impact by working to educate others about important votes.

2. **Pray for, volunteer with, or donate to your local pro-life women's health clinic (also sometimes known as a crisis pregnancy center).** These clinics provide a variety of counseling and medical services to women with unplanned pregnancies (for example, free pregnancy tests and ultrasounds), but do *not* offer abortion services or refer women to abortion providers. Their legitimacy is constantly under attack by pro-abortion organizations and websites accusing them of deception and misinformation for not promoting abortion services. In fact, it can be difficult to even find a local pro-life clinic using a search engine because they're often suppressed in search results. Ironically, you can sometimes most easily find one near you through one of several sites dedicated to warning women about them. Several of these sites have nationwide lists and will show up first when you search.

3. **Volunteer with a mobile pregnancy clinic or start one at your own church.** A mobile pregnancy clinic is like a women's health clinic on wheels (and often functions as the mobile arm of a women's health clinic). It travels within

a given geographic area to bring services more directly to women in crisis. You can volunteer with an existing mobile clinic or even start one as a ministry of your church. Save the Storks is an excellent organization that partners with churches to launch mobile clinics and much more (www. savethestorks.com). They report that 80 percent of women who board one of their busses choose life.

4. **Bring a speaker from the Life Training Institute (LTI) to your church, school, or event to help get more Christ-followers passionate about pro-life advocacy.** LTI's purpose is "to empower others with the knowledge and conviction necessary to make a case for life that changes hearts and minds." They've trained thousands of Christians since 2004. Go to www.prolifetraining.com.

5. **Host a pro-life book study group at your church or on your own.** Given that at least one-third of Christians are pro-choice (recall the statistics earlier in this chapter), much clarity is still needed in the church on abortion. In addition, many of those who *are* pro-life don't know how to defend their position. Even if your church isn't able to bring in a professional speaker to better equip your congregation, you can gather a group and study a pro-life book together. Choose one of the resources in the "Recommendations for Further Study" section at the end of this book.

6. **Create a fundraiser for a pro-life organization of your choosing.** You don't have to get fancy! Grab some friends and do something fun together to raise money your group can donate. If you have kids or work in youth ministry, this is also a great way to get a conversation started about why advocating for preborn life is so important.

7. **Buy products from companies committed to a pro-life position.** There are a variety of companies that explicitly state they are pro-life, and many even contribute a portion of their proceeds to pro-life causes. For example, search online for "pro-life diaper companies," "pro-life coffee companies," or "pro-life apparel companies." Most large corporations today are going out of their way to fund employees' abortions (including out-of-state travel costs). Whenever possible, use your dollars to support smaller companies committed to life.

CHAPTER 9

CRUEL RIGHTS-DENIERS

The View from Transgender Activists

■ ■ ■

J amie Bruesehoff is a lifelong Lutheran, a pastor's wife, and a mom to three kids. In a blog post titled, "My Transgender Daughter is a Beloved Child of God," she shares the story of her child Rebekah— at the time, a ten-year-old biological male happily living as a female.[1]

Bruesehoff recounts how her now joy-filled child wasn't always thriving. In the years before Rebekah "transitioned to live as [his] authentic self in the world," he had grown increasingly anxious, uncomfortable, and confused.[2] He fell into depression at age seven and wanted to die. Rebekah pushed the screen out of his second-floor window one day and tried to jump out. His parents were, of course, scared for his life and sought help from professionals. Bruesehoff says that's when the turning point happened:

> We all came to realize she wasn't a boy. She was a girl. At eight years old, we changed her name and pronouns and she began living as herself in the world. She immediately transformed into a confident, joyful child whose smile lights up an entire room.

By the time Bruesehoff wrote this blog post in 2017, Rebekah's story would have been pretty unshocking to many people—just as it was likely unshocking to you today. It's one of many stories that have been shared in blogs, articles, videos, and the mainstream media over the last few years that have a similar pattern: A child or adolescent exhibited a strong desire to be the opposite sex, grew increasingly distraught as he or she was expected to live as their biological sex (often to the point of becoming suicidal), was eventually allowed to live as the opposite sex by parents who had gained a deeper understanding of their child's struggles, and went on to live happily as their authentic (transgender) self.

But only *one* decade before Bruesehoff wrote her blog post, such stories were still novel.

For example, in 2007, a special edition of the primetime TV show *20/20* featured Barbara Walters interviewing three families with transgender children.[3,4] It's clear from the tone of the interviews that *20/20* assumed most of its viewers had very little exposure to transgender people or related issues. *Variety* magazine later called that episode a "watershed moment for transgender visibility" because of the subject's novelty at that time in the mainstream media.[5]

Fast-forward to today, and there are transgender influencers with millions of social media followers (including Jazz Jennings, who was one of the three kids featured in the *20/20* special when he was six years old). Ad campaigns for major companies feature transgender people, popular retail stores offer products designed for transgender buyers, the US celebrates a Transgender Day of Visibility every March, at least 579 state bills are in progress related to transgender issues at the time of this writing, and 42 percent of Americans say they now know someone who considers themself transgender.[6,7]

All in the span of two decades.

As transgender people, their stories, and their concerns have grown to widespread prominence, so has culture's demand for their unwavering affirmation. To not affirm the reality of people's ability to change genders and to not support the corresponding societal accommodations of such changes is now considered a cruel violence to the transgender community—a matter of life and death for people who are suffering and suicidal.

Just as with other topics featured in this book, Christians are among those most known and condemned for being at odds with the cultural consensus. Jaime Bruesehoff (again, herself a Lutheran) claims, for example, "People of faith are doing the loudest and most significant harm to [the transgender] community, personally and politically."[8]

In this chapter, we'll look at how transgender stories and related issues went from being novel in 2007 to prominent today—and not only prominent, but favored to the degree that anyone who doesn't believe a person can change genders is guilty of life-threatening harm to transgender people. I'll explain this seismic shift through the lens of two especially important drivers: definitions and numbers.

Definitions: From Mental Disorder to Identity

A little history sometimes tells a big story. Such is the case when you follow how the field of psychiatry has viewed gender-related diagnoses over time.

The Diagnostic and Statistical Manual of Mental Disorders, commonly known as the DSM, is the industry-standard reference book on mental health published by the American Psychiatric Association (APA). Five editions of the DSM have been published since 1952, with the most recent one (DSM-5) published in 2013. When the third edition (DSM-III) came out in 1980, gender-related diagnoses appeared for the first time in DSM history: transsexualism and Gender Identity Disorder of Childhood (GIDC) were listed in the Psychosexual Disorders category.

According to DSM-III, transsexualism referred to adults with a "persistent sense of discomfort and inappropriateness about one's anatomic sex and a persistent wish to be rid of one's genitals and to live as a member of the other sex."[9] GIDC referred to children with a similar sense of discomfort and "the desire to be, or insistence that he or she is, of the other sex." In both cases, the prevalence was noted as "rare."

Over the next several years, transgender activists became increasingly concerned about these new entries in the DSM, because inclusion in the DSM implied that wanting to or feeling the need to live as the opposite sex is a mental health problem in need of diagnosis and treatment. Many activists didn't want what they considered to be an *identity* stigmatized as a *mental illness*. At the same time, they realized that a diagnosis is typically required for access to the medical interventions necessary for gender transitions, so eliminating transgender-related entries from the DSM would be problematic as well.

The fourth edition of the DSM, published in 1994, did little to resolve these tensions. The APA only removed the term *transsexualism* and created a new single diagnosis for adults *and* kids called Gender Identity Disorder. Concerns continued, of course, because the name Gender Identity Disorder implies something is wrong—*disordered*—if a person identifies as a gender incongruent with their biological sex. Again, many transgender activists didn't see their gender identification as disordered at all. From their perspective, it was simply a function of who they were—an identity.

But a profound shift happened when DSM-5 came out in 2013.

For the first time, the DSM explicitly stated that "gender nonconformity is not in itself a mental disorder." Gender Identity Disorder was correspondingly replaced by Gender Dysphoria, a diagnosis representing only the "*psychological distress* that results from an incongruence between one's sex assigned at birth and one's gender identity" (emphasis added).[10] The APA's "Guide for Working with Transgender and Gender Nonconforming Patients" explains the significance of the diagnostic shift this way:

This change further focused the diagnosis on the gender
identity-related distress that some transgender people
experience (and for which they may seek psychiatric,
medical, and surgical treatments) rather than on transgender
individuals or identities themselves. The presence of gender
variance is not the pathology but dysphoria is from the
distress caused by the body and mind not aligning and/or
societal marginalization of gender-variant people.[11]

In other words, the persistent desire or felt need to live as a member
of the opposite sex was no longer considered a disorder to be treated,
but rather, an identity to be embraced. Only if a person *feels* distress
about gender incongruence is there a need for mental health treatment.

It would be hard to overemphasize the significance of this shift.
While there are numerous implications for what we're seeing in culture, there are three especially important ones I want to highlight
for our purposes here.

First, DSM-5 didn't cause *culture to begin thinking of being transgender as an identity, but it did give validation to existing ideological
trends.* Given that there were transgender activists already concerned
about "transsexualism" being included in DSM-III in 1980, it's clear
that some people's understanding of being transgender as an identity
(not a disorder) predated DSM-5. In fact, historian Carl Trueman
makes the case in his book *The Rise and Triumph of the Modern Self*
that the philosophical underpinnings of transgender identity claims
can be traced to cultural developments that have taken place over hundreds of years (and if you're interested in this depth of insight on the
subject, I highly recommend the book). But now that the APA has
formally stated that "gender non-conformity is not in itself a mental disorder," those who see being transgender as an identity have
what functions as an expert witness—if the main professional association of psychiatric experts says it's true, it must be true. Anyone

who disagrees that gender can be separated from biological sex is now looked at with contempt for holding archaic beliefs inconsistent with modern psychiatric science.

Second, the diagnosis of Gender Dysphoria implies that a person with feelings of gender incongruence needs help changing their body, not their mind. When these kinds of feelings were considered a mental disorder, therapy could be targeted at helping a person come to terms with their biological sex. The problem was the mind, not the body. But the shift to viewing being transgender as a mentally healthy identity now requires people to view the *body* as the problem. The culturally approved assumption is that transgender people know who their authentic self is and need a body to match what they know to be true (along with the social affirmation that their knowledge is accurate). Importantly, this assumption explains why any kind of therapy for the purpose of helping people change their *mind* rather than their *body* is now an abomination that's even being outlawed in many places. To suggest there's a need to change a person's mind is to suggest that people *aren't* the authority on who their true self is—or that, at the very least, they can sometimes be wrong. That's a deeply offensive idea in today's culture. So, in order to uphold the belief that every person determines who they are, everyone—including medical professionals—is now expected to unquestioningly affirm transgender feelings as corresponding to reality.

Third, when a person does feel gender-related mental distress, the blame is now largely placed on those who don't affirm their identity. The National Center for Transgender Equality, for example, says, "It's important to remember that while being transgender is not in itself an illness, many transgender people need to deal with physical and mental health problems because of widespread discrimination and stigma."[12] In other words, if society were fully accepting of transgender identities and provided the accommodations necessary to support those identities, transgender people wouldn't feel distress. So when they *do* feel distress, it reflects a problem with society, not the person. Thus, if you don't affirm that gender can be separated from biological sex, you're now seen as causing people to have a diagnosable mental illness.

Clearly, the shift to viewing being transgender as an identity has had far-reaching implications for society, especially for those who don't affirm that view. But there's one other major shift we need to understand before assessing all of this from a biblical perspective: the shift in numbers.

Numbers: The Transgender Explosion

As we just saw, much changed in the diagnostic approach from the time the DSM-III first described transsexualism in 1980 to the time the DSM-5 described Gender Dysphoria in 2013. One fact, however, remained the same over those years: *People with gender-related distress were exceedingly rare.* DSM-5 reported an expected incidence of gender dysphoria at .005-.014 percent for biological males and .002-.003 percent for biological females based on those seeking medical intervention at the time. Using the averages of those two ranges, that translates to about 1 in 10,000 males and 1 in 40,000 females.

Today, a little more than a decade later, the Pew Forum reports that 2 percent of adults ages 18-29 identify as transgender (200 per 10,000), .3 percent of those 30-49 (30 per 10,000), and .2 percent of those 50+ (20 per 10,000).[13,14] And for the first time in medical history, biological females make up a large number, and possibly the majority, of those identifying as transgender.[15]

Being transgender is no longer so rare—and no longer so biologically male. But why? Here, too, a little history tells a big story.

In her book *Irreversible Damage: The Transgender Craze Seducing Our Daughters*, Abigail Shrier recounts how Dr. Lisa Littman, an "obgyn turned public health researcher," stumbled onto something statistically bewildering one day in 2016.[16] Littman was scrolling through social media when she saw that a group of adolescent friends from her small town—mostly girls—had come out as transgender. Shrier recounts Littman's surprise that day: "Dr. Littman's curiosity snagged on the social media posts she'd seen. Why would a psychological ailment that had been almost exclusively the province of boys suddenly befall teenage girls? And why would the incidence of gender dysphoria be so much higher in friend clusters?"[17]

To answer these questions, Littman dug into the available scientific literature. *Before 2012, there was no scientific literature at all on girls ages 11 to 21 having developed gender dysphoria.*[18] Littman decided to conduct a study of her own. She gathered 256 detailed reports from parents with transgender-identifying adolescents who had no childhood history of gender dysphoria (prior to the last decade, symptoms of Gender Dysphoria were known to nearly always first appear in very early childhood—typically before age four). What she discovered was eye-opening:

> First, the clear majority (65 percent) of the adolescent girls who had discovered transgender identity in adolescence—"out of the blue"—had done so after a period of prolonged social media immersion. Second, the prevalence of transgender identification within some of the girls' friend groups was more than seventy times the expected rate.[19]

Littman realized something very different was happening relative to the "classic" Gender Dysphoria cases which were, again, exceedingly rare, predominantly male, and nearly always emerging in early childhood. *It appeared to be a form of peer contagion, driven by online influences.* She named the phenomenon rapid-onset gender dysphoria (ROGD) and published an academic paper with her findings. The paper became one of the most widely discussed academic articles of 2018…but not because people were grateful for her findings.

Transgender activists were furious and labeled Littman a bigot and a bully. They called her work dangerous and said it would lead to "worse mental health outcomes" for transgender adolescents.[20] The journal that published her paper even issued a rare apology.[21]

None of this should be surprising, of course. If it's assumed that being transgender is an identity based on a person's knowledge of their authentic self, then suggesting it might sometimes be nothing more than peer contagion is going to ruffle a lot of feathers—especially when this type of "transgenderism" accounts for a significant portion of the numbers explosion. It's a boon to the cause when so many new people are identifying as transgender, but devastating to the cause when it turns out they might simply be caught up in a fad.

But why would this be of interest to adolescent girls in the first place? Keep in mind, we're not talking about girls simply dressing more like boys for a couple of months because their friends are. We're talking about girls taking puberty-blocking hormones, seeking double mastectomies, and making other serious, life-altering decisions. If it's a social contagion, it's one that requires a profound commitment. So what's the incentive?

I've read no firsthand account that better answers that question than that of Helena Kirschner. Kirschner was 15 years old when she was introduced to transgender ideology on the social media and microblogging site Tumblr (transgender ideology meaning the worldview assumptions driving the idea that a person's gender can differ from their biological sex).[22] She began identifying as nonbinary, and by the time she was 18, she considered herself a transgender man. After a year and a half on testosterone, Kirschner realized she had caused a "disaster" for her health and decided to detransition (that is, make the social and physical changes still possible to live again as her biological sex).

In a detailed account of what first led her to seek a gender change, she explained how it was the critical theory–based social justice thinking we discussed in chapter 7. She no longer wanted to be seen as a "privileged" white, straight, "cisgender" person:

> You can't change your race, [and] pretending to have a different sexuality would be very uncomfortable in practice, but you can absolutely change your gender, and it's as easy as putting a "she/they" in your bio. Instantly you are transformed from an oppressing, entitled, evil, bigoted, selfish, disgusting [cisheterosexual] white scum into a valid trans person who deserves celebration and special coddling to make up for the marginalization and oppression you supposedly now face. Now not expected to do *as much* groveling...you can relax a little and talk about your life without wondering if you are distracting from the struggles of or speaking over marginalized groups, because you are marginalized too...This is the incentive I felt to comb through my thoughts and memories for things that might be further evidence that deep down, I wasn't really a girl.[23]

Many accounts like this one are now emerging as detransitioners share their stories. Adolescent girls struggling with social acceptance, depression, anxiety, and other mental health issues find a community online ready to embrace and celebrate them...as soon as they take on an "oppressed" identity (oppressed according to the neo-Marxist social binary). Desperate for attention and affirmation, they're willing to go to any length to be part of a marginalized group.[24] And gender is the one identity characteristic culture says you can actually change—as Kirschner said, stick a "she/they" in your bio, and you're on your way.

This isn't to suggest in any way that *every* adolescent girl identifying as transgender is *only* caught up in peer contagion or motivated to do it in order to be part of an oppressed group. But the numbers and stories emerging make it clear that these cases form a predictable pattern.[25] Critical theory–based social justice thinking has been the bus driving crowds of young girls to a presumed transgender utopia. Unfortunately, many are now looking back on the journey and realizing it delivered them to a nightmare.

All of that said, many people critiquing the transgender movement speak of ROGD as though it single-handedly accounts for the transgender explosion. But that's not the case. Relative to the expected incidence rate reported by DSM-III in 1980, the number of people identifying as transgender has skyrocketed in *every* age group for both biological males and females, in every racial/ethnic group, and in every state.[26] Yes, the numbers are disproportionately high among younger generations and adolescent girls in particular, but we're missing an important part of the bigger picture if we're looking *only* at ROGD.

Recall that in the beginning of this chapter, I said we'd look at the seismic cultural shift on transgender issues through the lens of two especially important drivers: definitions and numbers. Now that we've considered each one, it's crucial to note the connection. If there hadn't been such a growth in transgender numbers, the shift to culture viewing being transgender as an identity wouldn't have been so evident. It would likely have remained an issue of fringe significance to certain groups of activists. But at the same time, it's the shift to the identity view that *facilitated* the numbers explosion. Being transgender went from a mental disorder to a celebrated identity *due to the concurrent shift in critical theory–based social justice thinking.*

In other words, the redefinition of being transgender as an identity broke the dam and secular social justice ideology brought the flood. And it's a flood that lifted all boats:

- There are more young children today identifying as transgender because parents are now more likely to question their child's gender given the visibility of the subject in a culture that pervasively promotes secular social justice ideas.

- There are more school-age children identifying as transgender because many (if not most) public schools are teaching students as early as kindergarten that they may be a gender other than their biological sex. This encourages kids to explore gender in ways they may never have otherwise considered.

- There are more adolescent girls identifying as transgender due to the factors we discussed surrounding ROGD.

- There are more adolescent boys *and* girls identifying as transgender when feeling various kinds of discomfort with their bodies—some of which may be "classic" gender dysphoria and some of which may primarily be comorbid issues (for example, depression, anxiety, eating disorders, and autism have all been shown to have a high correlation in teens reporting feelings of gender incongruence).[27] With increased social acceptance and celebration comes an increased attribution of diverse issues to Gender Dysphoria.

- There are more people, both young and old, who are *willing* to identify as transgender when experiencing gender dysphoria given that there is now increased social acceptance.

In all of the above cases, culture is ready to receive, with open and affirming arms, anyone who questions their gender.

But how should Christians respond?

Three Truths Christians Must Understand

While this is a complex issue, ultimately, there are only three core truths that Christians must understand as a foundation for a biblically loving response for the common good.

1. Biological sex cannot be separated from gender.

As we've seen in this chapter, the heart of today's transgender ideology is the notion that individuals determine their identity and that one aspect they can determine is their gender (which may or may not line up with their biological sex).

According to Scripture, neither of these ideas is true.

One of the first facts established in the Bible is that God created humans. As created beings, we don't get to tell our Creator who we are and what our purpose is; we *receive* that information through what He's revealed in Scripture. Just 27 verses into Genesis, we're told that "God created man in his own image, in the image of God he created him; male and female he created them" (Genesis 1:27). Importantly, these male and female forms aren't incidental biological categories mentioned in passing. We learn from the rest of Scripture that they're essential to God's entire plan for humanity. Men and women are to come together in marriage as "one flesh" (Genesis 2:24). Because of their physical complementarity, they're able to fulfill the command to "be fruitful and multiply" (Genesis 1:28). And the relationship between a husband and wife is so important it's considered to be a picture of Christ's relationship to the church (Ephesians 5:31-32).

Furthermore, Scripture never envisions men and women as disembodied "genders" that can be separated from their bodies. Our bodies are a physical expression of maleness and femaleness. Ethics professor Andrew T. Walker helpfully summarizes the relationship this way:

> A person with male anatomy is reflecting physically the
> fact that they are created a man. A person with female

anatomy is reflecting that she is a woman. Maleness isn't
only anatomy, but anatomy shows there is maleness. And
femaleness isn't only anatomy, but anatomy shows there
is femaleness. Men and women are more than just their
anatomy, but they are not less. Our anatomy tells us what
gender we are.[28]

None of this means that people don't genuinely struggle with gender dysphoria. People struggle with all kinds of physical and mental
health problems due to the effects of the fall (Genesis 3), and Christians should treat those struggling with gender identity with the
same love and compassion as we would anyone else. But we need
to remember that if we're going to *truly* love transgender people in
a biblical sense, we need to advocate for what's objectively good for
them—even when it's not what they want for themselves. That brings
us to the second point.

2. Because biological sex cannot be separated from gender, "gender-affirming" medical and surgical procedures cause grave bodily harm to transgender people.

Because culture now views being transgender as a body problem,
medical and surgical procedures to alter the body are correspondingly considered to be the solution. This solution is euphemistically
labeled *gender-affirming care* and refers to the range of health services
provided to those who want to align characteristics of their physical
body with their transgender identity. Among the nonsurgical options
are puberty blockers, cross-sex hormones, and voice therapy. Surgical options include procedures such as breast removal, breast aug-
mentation, facial feminization, hysterectomy, vaginoplasty (creating
a vagina for biological men), and phalloplasty (creating a penis for
biological women).

These are clearly serious medical decisions. And they're considered to be the healthy, lifesaving response to gender dysphoria...when the body is assumed to be the problem.

But what if, as we've already seen biblically, the body *isn't* the problem? What if a person's body reflects their God-given gender as it should? What does *that* make these procedures?

Harmful. Destructive. Mutilating. Sterilizing.

That's not hyperbole.

Recall from chapter 2 that determining what's beneficial or harmful for a person or object depends on the purpose of that person or object. We saw that humans are created *for* something—to know God, love God, and make Him known. God has a design for human flourishing, including gender and sexuality, and that design facilitates the meeting of our objective purpose. Because "gender-affirming care" works against God's design, it can never be beneficial, no matter how much any individual may *feel* it is. Forcing a body to develop traits other than it was designed to have, removing healthy organs, or creating artificial organs that will never function the way real ones do will *only ever be harmful.*

But that doesn't mean transgender people don't need help. It doesn't mean we should tell them to get over it and get on with their lives because God knows best. God *does* know best, but sometimes people who are struggling with the challenges of living in a fallen world need a different kind of help. And that brings us to the third and final point.

3. Transgender people need truth-driven, compassionate mental health care.

This is where the subject is particularly difficult from an emotional perspective. Gender-affirming procedures are considered lifesaving because people with gender dysphoria report tragically high rates of suicidal ideation and suicide attempts. Because the body is presumed to be the problem that's causing suicidal thoughts or desires, "fixing" the body is presumed to be the lifesaving solution. Parents of children exhibiting gender dysphoria are consequently told that if they don't affirm their child's transgender identity, they'll soon have a dead child—an emotional blackmail of the most disturbing kind. Thus, if you don't support gender-affirming procedures—even for children and adolescents—culture will tell you that you literally have blood on your hands.

These are some emotionally weighty accusations, but we need to maintain biblical clarity of thought on how to respond. If someone you love were anorexic and threatened to take their own life if you didn't allow them to get liposuction, would you be willing to facilitate that process with your unwavering support? Would you believe you were being loving in doing so? Of course not. You know it would be harmful, and you would intuitively recognize that a need for liposuction isn't the problem—the problem is the mental state that led your loved one to think suicidally over their desire for liposuction in the first place. If this is obvious (and it should be), why is it not equally obvious when the example is replaced with gender dysphoria? Because (once again) culture presupposes that gender dysphoria is a body problem that needs to be fixed, so we mustn't get in the way of the help people need.

As Christians, we shouldn't support a culture-wide mutilation of healthy bodies in the name of loving transgender people any more than we should support culture-wide liposuction for anorexics—even when people so desperately feel the need to transition their gender that they're thinking of suicide. Research shows individuals with gender dysphoria exhibit elevated rates of depressive symptoms (64 percent), suicidality (43 percent), substance-use issues (40 percent), anxiety (26 percent), and general distress (34 percent) compared to the general population.[29] What mentally suffering people need is truth-driven, compassionate mental health care, not access to physical destruction.

The Transgender Explosion Affects Everyone

I know the subject of this chapter hits very close to home for some readers, whether they've personally struggled with gender dysphoria or have walked alongside a family member or friend who has. But even though 42 percent of Americans say they know a transgender person, that means the majority of Americans (and presumably readers of this book) still do not. So, if the subject hasn't touched you personally, I realize this can all sound theoretical. However, I assure you it's not.

The explosive growth in the number of people identifying as transgender affects everyone. *Not only do Christians need to properly care for individuals in our own lives who struggle with this issue, we need to care for the common good of a society that's promoting systemic changes to accommodate the destructive falsehoods of transgender ideology.*

Fortunately, many states are now actively working to limit that impact, and Christians should lead the way in voicing support accordingly. Legislative action on this subject began in 2015 with 21 bills, 14 of which were related to public restroom policies requiring people to use facilities corresponding with their biological sex.[30] From 2015 to 2019, nearly all transgender-related bills were of this nature.[31] But legislative activity quintupled by 2022 and then further tripled by 2024 with the growth of bills aimed at 1) maintaining the division of sports teams based on biological sex, 2) protecting minors from gender-affirming procedures (medical and/or surgical), and 3) establishing school district policies that protect parents and kids from the impact of transgender ideology in a variety of ways (more on that in the action points for this chapter).

Of course, these are all labeled *anti-trans rights* bills by transgender activists, but don't be fooled. From God's perspective, they are pro-the-good-of-transgender-people and pro-the-good-of-everyone-else bills. This legislative activity will likely continue to swell as certain states attempt to place limits on the harmful impact of transgender ideology. But be aware: Other states are effectively doubling down on the protection of transgender ideology over the protection of transgender people…and everyone else. They're passing bills to medically facilitate youth gender transitions, hide youth gender transitions from parents, promote transgender ideology in public schools at younger and younger ages, and much more. They'll do so in the name of rights, love, equality, protection, and human dignity.

But that's pulling the wool over your eyes.

Culture may be deceived by transgender ideology, but Christians can't sheepishly play along. When we follow the Good Shepherd, we must boldly follow His voice and His alone (John 10:27). Doing so is the only way to truly love transgender people—no matter how much culture claims otherwise.

QUICK RESPONSES TO 5 POPULAR CHALLENGES
on Transgender Issues

1. No matter how much you refuse to accept it, transgender people exist.

(Questions: What do you mean by exist? Why do you think I don't believe transgender people exist?)

No one denies that people exist who believe they're a gender other than that which corresponds with their biological sex. However, that's different than believing people exist whose gender is *actually* different from their biological sex. As a Christian, I don't believe gender can be separated from biological sex because the Bible teaches God created each person male or female, and our bodies reflect that God-ordained design even when individuals sometimes feel otherwise.

2. If you believe in God, you should believe God made transgender people the way they are and let them live as their authentic selves.

(Questions: Do you believe in God? If so, what is your source of knowledge about Him and what He wants for people? How do you know that a transgender person's authentic self is reflected by what they think rather than by their physical body? Can someone ever be wrong about who they are? Why or why not?)

I don't merely believe in a creator God—I believe in a God who has revealed, in the Bible, the truth about who He is, who we are, and the way the world is. The Bible teaches that God created each person male or female and that our physical bodies reflect that God-ordained design. From a biblical perspective, a person's true or authentic self—including their gender—is defined by God, not by the individual.

3. Your condemnation is what causes transgender people to commit suicide.

(Questions: What do you mean by condemnation? How did you come to the conclusion that this is the reason transgender people want to commit suicide rather than any factors relating to themselves?)

There's no question that some people suffer deeply due to feelings that their gender is at odds with their biological sex, and sometimes they suffer to the degree that they want to take their own life. But people struggling with gender dysphoria need compassionate mental health care, not affirmation of false beliefs. Just as we wouldn't encourage someone with anorexia to eat less under the false belief they're overweight, we shouldn't encourage someone with gender dysphoria to make destructive changes to their body under the false belief they're a gender that doesn't align with their biological sex.

4. Trans rights are human rights.

(Questions: Which rights do you believe transgender people should have that they don't currently have? Why do you believe they're entitled to those rights?)

Human rights are rights to which every person is entitled by their Creator and are based on equality in human value and dignity. But equality in human value and dignity doesn't imply that the government must give transgender people every right they seek. *No one* is entitled to every right they seek simply because they're human.

5. Intersex people prove there are more than two genders.

(Questions: Why do you believe the fact that some people have disorders of sex development shows there are more than two genders?)

Intersex conditions are *disorders* of male/female sex development, not the development of a third sex. This is unrelated to transgender issues, where sex development is normal, but a person *feels* like they're the opposite sex.

ACTIONS FOR THE COMMON GOOD:
7 Ways to Shine Your Light Through
Transgender Issues

1. **Make your voice heard with your elected representatives on transgender-related bills in progress.** Of greatest prominence and significance right now are bills limiting gender-affirming medical and surgical procedures for youth. In April 2021, Arkansas became the first state to limit such actions. Two more states followed in 2022, and then 19 states followed in 2023.[32] It's encouraging that more and more states are recognizing the harm being done to kids in the name of "lifesaving" care. Find out what your state is doing and get involved accordingly (including the *opposition* of bills designed to protect gender-affirming procedures for youth).

2. **Gather information on how your local school district handles gender-related issues and bring concerns to your school board.**[33] A valuable site for resources on how to do so is childparentrights.org. The following are examples of policies being implemented in concerned districts across America:

   - *School curriculum transparency.* These policies require educators to seek permission from parents before teaching topics related to gender identity or sexuality.

   - *Parental disclosure rules.* These policies require school staff to inform a student's parents if the student shows signs that they're identifying as transgender (for example, going by a different name or using pronouns that don't align with their biological sex). While you may assume that this would already be basic school policy, it's not in many places. In fact, there have been several high-profile cases involving schools that have gone to great lengths to hide a student's transition from their parents.[34]

- *Sex-based designations for school facilities.* These policies require students to use bathrooms and locker rooms that align with their biological sex.

- *Sex-based school sports.* These policies require students to participate on sports teams that align with their biological sex.

3. **Refuse to participate in pronoun declarations.** People are now regularly being asked to state their pronouns in email signatures for work, on job applications, at conferences, in medical settings, and in many other environments. But asking for pronouns assumes that transgender ideology corresponds with reality, and therefore every person needs to identify their gender because it may not be the same as their biological sex. As such, to declare your pronouns is to tacitly participate in the promotion of a false worldview. The more that Christians and others who reject this ideology speak up, the more difficult it will become for organizations to impose this falsehood on others. For a sample response to an employer's pronoun request, see the source cited in this endnote.[35]

4. **Speak up when companies promote transgender ideology.** When companies promote transgender ideology through their ads, products in their retail stores, or supportive online messaging, take the time to say something (Pantene, Gillette, Adidas, Bud Light, Nike, and Target are all high-profile

examples of such companies from the last few years). Reach out through customer channels to voice your concerns graciously and let them know you'll be spending your money elsewhere (if applicable).

5. **Take the opportunity to spend time with a transgender person and hear about their experiences firsthand.** While it's critical for Christians to think rightly about transgender ideology, we can't forget that we're not merely talking about ideas, we're talking about people. If you're acquainted with someone who identifies as transgender, ask them if they'd be willing to share about their gender experiences over lunch. Get to know them. Listen to their story. Talking with a transgender person will help you engage on this issue from a more personal perspective. If you aren't acquainted personally with someone who is transgender, read Laura Perry Smalts's book *Transgender to Transformed: A Story of Transition That Will Truly Set You Free.*[36]

6. **Speak to the youth group in your church or other churches about gender from a biblical perspective.** Because teens are particularly exposed to transgender ideology, they're an especially important group to reach. Develop a talk to educate the youth at your church on gender from a biblical perspective and how that differs from the transgender ideology so popular today. Because many teens now have school classmates who identify as transgender, be sure to discuss what it means to love transgender friends without affirming their transgender identity.

7. **Start a ministry at your church to reach transgender and/or detransitioning people.** I realize this action point is a huge one that very few people are likely to consider. However,

I'm including it here because I believe there's a significant ministry gap in this area. It's estimated that there are more than one million transgender people in the United States, and very, very few Christian ministries exist to reach them. In fact, when you search online for "Christian transgender ministries," the top search results are sadly for churches affirming people in their transgender identity. If you have the desire and ability to reach people struggling with gender-related issues, talk to your church leadership and consider what you can do.

CHAPTER 10

HATEFUL BIGOTS

The View from the Sexual Revolution

■ ■ ■

In 1987, Marshall Kirk partnered with advertising executive Hunter Madsen to write an essay for *Guide* magazine called "The Overhauling of Straight America."[1] The essay was a marketing strategy for getting straight people to think about gay people in more positive ways. Kirk and Madsen bluntly wrote:

> The first order of business is desensitization of the American public concerning gays and gay rights. To desensitize the public is to help it view homosexuality with indifference instead of with keen emotion. Ideally, we would have straights register differences in sexual preference the way they register different tastes for ice cream or sports games: she likes strawberry and I like vanilla; he follows baseball and I follow football. No big deal.
>
> At least in the beginning, we are seeking public desensitization and nothing more…If only you can get them to think that it is just another thing, with a shrug of their shoulders, then your battle for legal and social rights is virtually won.

Kirk and Madsen detailed six strategic steps for meeting these goals (their words, not mine): 1) Talk about gays and gayness as loudly and as often as possible; 2) portray gays as victims, not as aggressive challengers; 3) give protectors a just cause; 4) make gays look good; 5) make the victimizers look bad; and 6) solicit funds. They later more fully developed these ideas in their 1990 book *After the Ball: How America Will Overcome Its Fear and Hatred of Gays in the 90s.*[2]

If ever there were a stated marketing strategy that could be deemed successful in retrospect, it's this. After all, same-sex marriage was legalized in 2015, and culture overwhelmingly embraces all things LGBTQ today. Kirk and Madsen's quest for "public desensitization" ended not merely with their desired cultural shrug of the shoulders but with celebratory pride parades—a far greater marketing outcome than even they envisioned. Christians and others who haven't gotten on board with the celebration are labeled *hateful bigots* and *homophobes*, just as step 5 in their marketing strategy prescribed.[3]

In many ways, the marketing campaign for the acceptance of homosexuality can be marked complete and successful. But there's a related campaign that's still going on and has yet to achieve the same level of cultural acceptance: *the campaign for the sexual liberation of children.*

You're probably at least somewhat aware that children are being targeted with LGBTQ content today in areas like children's entertainment and public-school sexual education. On a cursory level, you may think that things like these are merely an extension of the ongoing campaign for broad LGBTQ acceptance—that activists naturally want acceptance from everyone, and that would include kids. There is, of course, truth to that. But there's something else going on today that Christians need to understand: *The goal for a subset of LGBTQ activists is to free children from the sexual restrictions placed on them by society's norms, values, and expectations.*

That's a very different goal than convincing people of all ages that homosexuality is "just another thing," as Kirk and Madsen put it.

Many books have been written on LGBTQ issues and Christianity, but this more nuanced aspect of the subject receives far less attention, so I've chosen to focus specifically on it here. In this chapter, we'll see why LGBTQ activism and the quest for the sexual liberation of children are intimately connected movements and how they're impacting children today.

The Sexual Revolution and Children

While we can't cover every driving force behind the sexual revolution and its impact on children, we're going to focus on three especially important forces in twentieth-century history that have shaped what's happening today: Sigmund Freud, Alfred Kinsey, and queer theory.

Sigmund Freud

Our first stop is the father of psychoanalysis, Sigmund Freud (1856–1939).

For Freud, the primary goal of human existence was to be happy. This certainly wasn't a novel idea in the course of history, but Freud is known for connecting happiness specifically with sexual pleasure. He wrote, for example:

> Man's discovery that sexual (genital) love afforded him the strongest experiences of satisfaction and in fact provided him with the prototype of all happiness, must have suggested to him that he should continue to seek the satisfaction of happiness in his life along the path of sexual relations and that he should make genital eroticism the central point of his life.[4]

Consider the implications of a culture making genital eroticism the central point of life:

1. Sex and sexual pleasure become central to what it means to be human—synonymous with our very identity;

2. sexual pleasure will take priority over all else, because if we're not sexually satisfied, we can't be fully happy;

3. most moral and legal restrictions on sexual freedom become harmful barriers to happiness that must be eradicated.[5]

Sound familiar? If Freud were alive today, I'm sure he would be more than pleased that culture has overwhelmingly embraced precisely these ideas. They underlie much of the LGBTQ movement. What isn't so obvious, however, is the implications these same ideas have for *children*.

If human identity is fundamentally sexual in nature, that implies we're sexual beings from birth. Indeed, for Freud, the central feature of each stage of human development was the type of sexual desire and satisfaction to be found at that stage. Yes, this even applies to infants. Freud's first stage of development was the oral stage, during which sexual pleasure is supposedly found through breastfeeding and thumb-sucking. The oral stage was followed by the anal, phallic, latency, and genital stages (the genital stage being all years from puberty to death). In this view, the process of growing up is inherently a process of progressing through stages of sexual pleasure-seeking behavior.

Much more could be said, but this suffices to explain how Freud left the world with a devastating and history-shaping theory: Human identity is essentially sexual in nature and that logically extends to even the youngest humans. Children are therefore just as sexual in nature as adults, and they, too, should be encouraged to explore their sexuality in the pursuit of happiness.

Alfred Kinsey

Alfred Kinsey was a sexologist and biologist who wrote two of the most influential books of the twentieth century: *Sexual Behavior in the Human Male* (1948) and *Sexual Behavior in the Human Female* (1953). Together, these books are known as the Kinsey Reports and have sold nearly one million copies.[6] You may not have heard of them, but you're living in a culture that's living out their implications every day.

The Kinsey Reports were purportedly scientific descriptions of the sexual practices of average Americans, based on Kinsey's research. Kinsey and his colleagues had collected thousands of interviews with people who provided detailed information about their sexual experiences. What he found was that people were far more sexually active and "adventurous" than anyone at the time would have imagined—a majority of white men were having sex with prostitutes, half of married men were cheating on their wives, and 37 percent of men had "at least some overt homosexual experience" (to name just a few of many findings).[7] Kinsey concluded that his work provided "a good opportunity for understanding the futility of classifying individuals as normal or abnormal, or well-adjusted or poorly adjusted, when in reality they may be nothing more than frequent or rare, or conformists or non-conformists with the socially pretended custom."[8]

In other words, the Kinsey Reports suggested to the world that people's sexual desires and experiences were far more varied than "repressive" social norms (such as heterosexuality) would suggest; what polite society considered deviant wasn't deviant at all. Kinsey's findings were the validation and permission culture needed to start throwing out presumed norms and living in sexual freedom. LGBTQ activists have used Kinsey's data for decades now to make the case that homosexuality is far more prevalent than anyone realizes.

What people didn't know—and often still don't—is that Kinsey's findings were based on an extremely flawed methodology. To give just a few examples, he significantly overrepresented prisoners, prostitutes, and homosexuals in his sample, relied on volunteer subjects who were more likely to report varied sexual experiences, and gathered data from child molesters.

The fact that Kinsey gathered data from child molesters is especially relevant to our present focus on children.[9] From this data, he cataloged 317 observations about children of every age from two months to adolescence having orgasms.[10] Kinsey believed that "these data on the sexual activities of younger males provide an important substantiation of the Freudian view of sexuality as a component that is present in the human animal from earliest infancy."[11]

There's the connection in Kinsey's own words. Freud provided the theory that human identity is fundamentally sexual in nature from infancy on, and Kinsey provided the "scientific" data to validate it. In addition, Kinsey went to great lengths to make the case that the recorded orgasms weren't simply a physiological response of a nonerotic nature. He referenced observational details from the 317 children to explicitly claim they had experienced "true orgasm."[12]

Thus, according to Kinsey, children are sexual beings who not only experience sexual responses but *enjoy* those responses. For him, the only reason children weren't normally engaging in sexual behavior was the existence of unnecessarily inhibiting social norms. Kinsey's thinking can be summarized by his own words in this statement: "It is difficult to understand why a child, *except for its cultural conditioning*, should be disturbed at having its genitalia touched, or disturbed at seeing the genitalia of other persons, or disturbed at even more specific sexual contacts" (emphasis added).[13]

Queer Theory

Our final stop in history isn't with a person but with a philosophy. And it's one we already discussed briefly in chapter 7: queer theory.

As a quick reminder, queer theory is the branch of critical theory that claims cisgender and heterosexual people are oppressively imposing cisheteronormativity on those in the LGBTQ community (cisheteronormativity being norms of gender and sexuality). Queer theorists claim that the categories of male/female and heterosexual/homosexual are merely social constructs that don't correspond to any essential truth independent of society's beliefs.

In order to understand the implications of queer theory, it's crucial to remember that *queer*, in this context, doesn't mean gay, as the term has sometimes been pejoratively used. *Queer* means any way of being that's at odds with what society considers to be normal. As such, *queer theory* isn't a broad term for the promotion of LGBT issues as the name might at first seem to imply. It very specifically promotes the destruction of *norms* related to gender and sexuality—which is not necessarily advocated by everyone who identifies as gay or transgender. A person can identify as gay or transgender, for example, and believe the gender binary of male and female (a societal norm) is a biological reality rather than a social construct to be dismantled.

So how does this relate to children? Well, let's take queer theory to its logical conclusions. One norm of mainstream American society is the belief that it's abusive for adults to involve children in sexual acts because children aren't sexual. I say *mainstream* society because, as we already saw, Freud began challenging that assumption more than a century ago. Freud, Kinsey, and others have promoted ideas to the contrary, but culture still overwhelmingly believes that adult-child sexual contact is wrong.

But that's a norm. And you should know at this point what queer theorists think of norms related to gender and sexuality. They have to go. Believing that there's something inherently wrong with adult-child sexual contact is allegedly one more way cisheteronormative societies oppress the natural, healthy sexual desires of both adults and children.

You might think that I'm merely working out logical conclusions that queer theorists themselves wouldn't acknowledge, but that's not the case. Examples extend back to what's widely considered to be the movement's founding document—a 1984 essay by Gayle Rubin called "Thinking Sex," in which Rubin wrote with great empathy for pedophiles. She lamented, "Like communists and homosexuals in the 1950s, boylovers [pedophiles] are so stigmatized that it is difficult to find defenders for their civil liberties, let alone for their erotic orientation."[14]

As a more recent example, associate professor Hannah Dyer at the University of Toronto argues that the concept of "childhood innocence" is a social construct that suppresses the possibility of a child expressing queerness and protects the assumption that a child will eventually become heterosexual.[15] Translation: If children are kept from exploring gender and sexuality at a young age under the assumption that they're "innocent"—that is, not sexual by nature—they'll be less likely to eventually develop a queer identity; they need to explore sexuality while young in order to not head down society's default path of cisheteronormativity. Dyer explicitly states she is interested in "understanding the possibility for children and youth to recruit amounts of bodily pleasure."[16] *According to activists like Dyer, then, early intervention is key to the so-called queering of children, including the opportunity to give them sexual agency.*

In short, because queer theory claims that all norms relating to gender and sexuality are merely social constructs, that means norms relating to children and sexuality are merely social constructs as well. Once activists successfully dismantle those "oppressive" norms, children will be free to express their inherently sexual nature.

Marketing Sexual Liberation to Kids

Now that we've looked at three of the important driving forces in the sexual revolution, we can summarize their ideas as follows, especially as they relate to children (note how they build on each other over time):

- **Freud:** Human identity is essentially sexual in nature, and that logically extends to even the youngest humans. Your sexuality is *who you are*. Children are therefore just as sexual in nature as adults, and they, too, should be encouraged to explore their sexuality in the pursuit of happiness. Societal restrictions on sexuality repress the true self for both adults and children.

- **Kinsey:** Children are sexual beings who not only experience sexual responses but also enjoy those responses. The only reason children aren't normally engaging in sexual behavior is the existence of unnecessarily inhibiting social norms.

- **Queer theory:** Gender *and* sexuality norms are merely social constructs, so gender and sexuality norms for *children* are merely social constructs as well. Once those "oppressive" norms are dismantled, children will be free to express themselves queerly.

Here's the tricky part: Culture to date has overwhelmingly accepted these ideas as they apply to adults, but it hasn't yet overwhelmingly accepted the same ideas as they apply to children. This poses both a challenge and opportunity for the subset of LGBTQ activists who want culture to accept *both* sides of the coin: Yes, the ideas they're promoting are still quite taboo, but some Kirk and Madsen–style marketing moves can make use of the shiny, culturally accepted side of the coin to usher in the dark underside.

And that's exactly what's going on.

The average person who broadly embraces LGBTQ ideas today assumes that related content for kids is merely about teaching them kindness, diversity, inclusion, and tolerance (for convenience, I'll refer to this group going forward as "mainstream allies"). Mainstream allies aren't part of the LGBTQ community themselves, but they enthusiastically support the cause in the name of justice and are oftentimes the most vocal group condemning those who don't affirm LGBTQ morality. They're "protectors" with a "just cause," as Kirk and Madsen sought in step 3 of their marketing strategy. Mainstream allies are the perfect tool for activists who want culture to embrace something more.

Let's look at a case study of how that happens.

Chances are, you've heard a lot about drag queens over the last few years due to the emergence in 2015 of Drag Queen Story Hour (DSH)—events in which drag queens read books on LGBTQ themes to young children in public libraries or other public spaces across the country.[17] Drag queens are performers (usually gay men) who dress in women's clothing, wear exaggerated women's makeup, and perform a variety of musical or comedy acts for audiences, typically of a sexual nature when in an adult context.

In any mainstream media article, you'll find drag queen events for children portrayed as sweet-as-candy occasions with performers reading "family-friendly" books and doing silly dances—simply a "safe space for reading and creativity," as one drag queen described it.[18] Parents who are mainstream allies enthusiastically line up to give their children the experience of learning about diversity and inclusion from fun performers who supposedly epitomize what it means to be true to yourself.

One mom, for example, made a tongue-in-cheek TikTok video on the "shocking truth" of what she observed when she took her young daughters to a drag brunch. The video laughingly shared how the children dressed in sparkles, put on makeup, and danced to kids' songs, all to purportedly show how ridiculous it is to think drag queens are somehow "traumatic" for kids. One of the video commenters similarly mocked, "Imagine, having kids dance to [the song 'Baby Shark']. No doubt they'll be traumatized forever."[19]

Parents like these have been completely fooled.

As mainstream allies, they *think* they're simply showing support to the LGBTQ community and raising kids to do the same. It's just sparkles, dancing, and reading, right?

Activists themselves will tell you that's not what these kinds of shows are for.

Drag queen Harris Kornstein, who goes by the drag name Lil Miss Hot Mess, sits on the board of DSH. Kornstein coauthored a surprisingly revealing academic article on the DSH movement titled "Drag pedagogy: The playful practice of queer imagination in early childhood."[20] The word *pedagogy* means the method and practice of teaching; thus, drag pedagogy is the process of teaching through drag. So what is it that they want to teach?

Kornstein and his coauthor Harper Keenan provide the answer to that very explicitly: "Ultimately, we suggest that drag pedagogy offers one model for learning not simply about queer lives, but how to live queerly." Contrary to the assumptions of most mainstream allies, the purpose isn't to teach kids about those who may be different from them, but rather, to teach kids to *become like them*—to live queerly themselves, resisting all norms of gender and sexuality from a young age.

Kornstein and Keenan explicitly see drag as an alternative form of education for children who are otherwise "straightened" into a heteronormative vision in their traditional schools:

> Building in part from queer theory and trans studies, queer and trans pedagogies seek to actively destabilize the normative function of schooling through transformative education…This is a fundamentally different orientation than movements towards the inclusion or assimilation of LGBT people into the existing structures of school and society.

By their own admission here, these programs are "fundamentally different" than the traditional push for LGBTQ "inclusion" that most mainstream allies assume they're participating in. Kornstein and Keenan go so far as to admit that they knowingly use language designed to attract the mainstream and keep their true goals in the shadows. For example, they say:

> It may be that DQSH is "family friendly," in the sense that it is accessible and inviting to families with children, but it is less a sanitizing force than it is a preparatory introduction to alternate modes of kinship. Here, DQSH is "family friendly" in the sense of "family" as an old-school queer code to identify and connect with other queers on the street.

So they'll tell you it's family friendly, and you can take from that what you will, but what they *really* mean is they want to prepare kids to be part of another kind of family—a queer family.

In another admission of the bait-and-switch strategy, they say, "It is undeniable that DQSH participates in many [tropes] of empathy, from the marketing language the programme uses to its selection of books. Much of this is strategically done in order to justify its educational value." Here again, they know they have to make use of their mainstream allies' desire to teach empathy in order to promote ideas that are currently less commonly accepted: dismantling gender and sexuality norms from an early age. This dismantling of norms is the preparatory work needed to achieve the sexual "liberation" of children.

I've taken the time to look at drag performances here in some depth because Kornstein and Keenan's paper offers a surprisingly honest and explicit lens through which to understand activists' objectives and marketing strategy. But drag is just one of several significant examples today of how activists are using the mainstream acceptance of LGBTQ ideology for adults to more subtly work toward the acceptance of sexual liberation for children. We don't have space to explore other examples as deeply, but I want to at least briefly note three other major ways this is currently happening:

1. **Comprehensive Sexuality Education:** Much of the sexual education in public schools today is rooted in a program called Comprehensive Sexuality Education (CSE). CSE claims to give young people accurate, age-appropriate information about sexuality, but it's thoroughly steeped in queer theory and is being pushed to kids as young as preschool age. CSE materials normalize and glamorize youth sex and experimentation in the name of inclusion—once again giving mainstream allies a just cause to protect. For an in-depth look at queer theory and its pervasiveness in the educational system, I highly recommend Logan Lancing and James Lindsay's book *The Queering of the American Child: How a New School Religious Cult Poisons the Minds and Bodies of Normal Kids.*[21]

2. **Books in school and public libraries:** There are a number of books for kids of all ages that are promoted by LGBTQ activists in school and public libraries. While mainstream allies see them as needed LGBTQ representation, many of these books are so sexually explicit (in language and even pictures) that they can easily be labeled *pornographic*— clearly designed to awaken children's sexuality. In the action points for this chapter, I'll note how to research what's in your local libraries and follow up accordingly.[22]

3. **Pride parades and similar events:** Pride parades are increasingly being billed as "family friendly." This, of course, brings in mainstream allies, but pride parades and events like them are typically highly sexual in nature. One "family friendly" parade, for example, had two men perform a sex

act in public.[23] While children aren't the main audience for such events, labeling them *family-friendly* intentionally encourages children of all ages to attend and subsequently exposes them to overtly sexual content.

I'm pretty confident that Christian readers of this book don't need to be convinced that children shouldn't be sexualized. Nonetheless, I want to close this chapter by comparing biblical teachings with the foundational claims of the sexual revolution to help readers think systematically about how to understand and respond to today's activism—as it relates to both adults and children.

Identity and Sexuality: The Bible vs. the Sexual Revolution

Recall from chapter 2 that there are three core biblical answers to the question of human identity: 1) Every human is made in the image of God; 2) every human has an objective purpose; and 3) every human has a sin nature. Let's work out the implications of these truths as they relate to the claims of the sexual revolution.

1. Every human is made in the image of God.

This point alone has two important implications that separate biblical truths about identity from the claims of the sexual revolution.

The first implication of the fact that every human is made in the image of God is that we are, indeed, made—we're created beings. As we discussed in chapter 9, if God created us, it logically follows that He has the authority and knowledge to tell us who we are. Because God revealed in Scripture the truths we need to know about ourselves, we have an objective source for that information, and it's independent of anything we might *feel* about our identity. *We can be wrong about who we are.*

The sexual revolution, on the other hand, is based on the presupposition that we either have no creator who has the authority to tell us who we are (an atheistic view) or that we have no creator who has *told* us who we are (a deistic view).[24] Thus, from this perspective, the ultimate authority on a person's identity lies in the subjective feelings of the self. There's no objective standard against which those feelings can be compared, so a person can never be wrong about who they are.

The second implication of the fact that every human is made in the image of God is that humans are inherently different in nature from animals—we are made in the image of God, but animals are not. As we saw in chapter 2, that means we're uniquely moral creatures who are able to reflect, reason, and make the choices necessary to execute the dominion that God gave us over the earth. Unlike animals, we are more than our biological instincts; God gave us a moral law and corresponding conscience to point us toward what is objectively good, and He has expectations of us accordingly (Romans 2:15). This is why we don't gasp in moral horror when a lion kills and eats an antelope, but we do when a human kills and eats another human.

The sexual revolution, however, is the logical outworking of naturalistic evolutionary assumptions that all living creatures—including humans—developed from a single-celled common ancestor. Given those assumptions, we as humans are not inherently different in our identity from animals. We have biological instincts and should be free to follow those instincts because that's what's *natural* to us. NBCUniversal, for example, honored Pride Month 2024 with a new nature documentary series called *Queer Planet*, in which it celebrated the "queerness" of the animal kingdom. The description of the documentary says:

> Take a worldwide journey exploring the rich diversity of animal sexuality—from flamboyant flamingos to pansexual primates, sex-changing clownfish, multi-gendered mushrooms and everything in between. This documentary looks at extraordinary creatures, witnesses

amazing behaviors, and introduces the scientists who are questioning the traditional concept of what's natural when it comes to sex and gender.[25]

It's not a coincidence that a documentary in support of the sexual revolution would look to the animal kingdom to determine what's *acceptable* through what's *natural*. If humans are merely animals without a moral lawgiver to differentiate between instincts and morality, then a sex-changing clownfish might tell us something about gender categories and a "pansexual" primate might tell us something about sexuality. In this view, if animals are driven by sexual instincts, we must be too.

2. Every human has an objective purpose.

As we established in chapter 2, we were created *for* something. We might think we have another purpose, but, once again, we can be wrong because the Creator is the one with the authority and ability to tell us the purpose for which He created us. Scripture says that God desires our steadfast love and knowledge of Him (Hosea 6:6) and our corresponding love of others (Luke 10:27). He desires that we know Jesus (John 17:3) and that all people would be saved and come to a knowledge of the truth (1 Timothy 2:4). In short, we are made to know God, love God, and make Him known to others.

In addition, God has a design for human flourishing to facilitate the fulfillment of this purpose—including a design for gender and sexuality. We already established in chapters 7 and 9 that God created people male and female. These categories are therefore not social constructs as claimed by the sexual revolution. This is important to understand because the reality of biological sexes underlies the biblical view of sexuality as well. Per our chapter 9 discussion, males and females are to come together in the unity of marriage, and the Bible repeatedly condemns sexual behavior outside of marriage between a man and a woman.[26] God designed sex specifically for the physical, spiritual, and emotional union between a husband and wife. And because sex is designed for marriage, no one—including children—should engage in sex outside of that context.

The sexual revolution makes two very different claims about purpose: 1) Our purpose is to maximize happiness, and 2) sexual fulfillment is central to maximizing happiness. These ideas, of course, logically flow from an uncreated, animal-based view of humanity. Creatures that are purely instinct-driven will seek whatever brings them the most pleasure without needing to exhibit moral restraint. Sexual pleasure is one of the strongest urges creatures have, so if one's purpose is to maximize happiness, sexual pleasure will naturally be a central component—even in the life of a child.

3. Every human has a sin nature.

The Bible teaches that every human has a sin nature—a desire to rebel against God and go our own way. Paul says in Ephesians 2:3 that before coming to Christ, all of us "lived in the passions of our flesh, carrying out the desires of the body and the mind, and were by nature children of wrath, like the rest of mankind." In other words, we are by nature pleasure-maximizers. Ironically, the Bible agrees with the sexual revolution in this! The disagreement is in whether that's descriptive or prescriptive—whether it describes what we do by nature or prescribes what we *should* do. The Bible acknowledges it's what we do by nature but teaches that there's a moral law that's greater than our instincts; it's not what we *should* do.

From the perspective of the sexual revolution, however, we're literally defined by our strongest instinct: We *are* sexual beings. Note that that's different than saying we're creatures with sexual instincts. It's saying our sexual instincts are our very essence. Sin isn't a consideration because God isn't in the picture. If following your instincts makes you happy, that's what you should do.

Clearly, the Bible and the sexual revolution are at great odds. And, as you can see, it's about far more than the verses in the Bible that directly address homosexuality. It's a fundamental disagreement about the very nature of mankind.

LGBTQ Activism and the Sexual Liberation of Children: Hand-in-Glove Movements

Nothing in this chapter suggests that everyone who identifies as LGBTQ wants to sexualize kids. In fact, there are groups of people in the LGBTQ community who understand the nature of the sexual revolution, see how activists are extending the ideas to kids, and are consciously and proactively rejecting that extension.[27] The quest for the sexual liberation of children is also not exclusively a subset of LGBTQ activism; you can find people promoting such ideas in varied places. But that said, the preponderance of activism for the sexual liberation of children is attached to LGBTQ activism.

If you understood the history presented in this chapter, that should make perfect sense. The sexual revolution facilitated the cultural acceptance of LGBTQ ideology by convincing culture that your identity is in your sexuality, so any sexual expression is valid because your desires are simply who you are. The nature of this thinking logically implies that the same conclusions are applicable to humans of any age. The movements fit together like a hand and glove.

This is also the key to understanding why culture hates Christians who fight against the sexualization of children through LGBTQ-connected initiatives like Drag Queen Story Hour or Comprehensive Sexuality Education. It's not that most people in culture are fighting for the sexualization of children—it's that they think Christians are fighting *against LGBTQ people*. Remember, the mainstream allies are often unaware of how certain LGBTQ-connected initiatives are being used to promote the sexual liberation of children.

In addition, the nature of the sexual revolution explains why culture hates anyone who doesn't accept LGBTQ ideas in the first place. If you presuppose that a person's sexual behavior is literally who they are, then the rejection of the morality of that behavior is seen as a harmful and hateful rejection of the whole person.

Christians, of course, aren't rejecting people. In advocating for societal righteousness in connection with gender and sexuality, whether for adults or children, we're affirming God's design *for* people. It's *for* the common good—a good defined, of course, by God. But that's a very tough distinction to communicate in today's culture. There's a sexual revolution stretching back more than a century that's convinced people otherwise.

QUICK RESPONSES TO 5 POPULAR CHALLENGES
on Sexuality

1. Christians are hateful bigots.

(Questions: How did you come to that conclusion? What do you mean by bigots? Can you give me some examples of when you've seen Christians act in hateful ways toward people in the LGBTQ community?)

While there have been some high-profile examples of people in the church saying terrible, derogatory things about the LGBTQ community, that's not consistent with Jesus's command for Christians to love others, and Christians should be the first to condemn that behavior. That said, loving others doesn't mean agreeing with them on everything they believe and do. Christians can love LGBTQ people while at the same time believing God has a design for gender and sexuality that's at odds with many LGBTQ beliefs and behaviors.

2. Christians are harming LGBTQ people by not accepting them for who they are.

(Questions: From your perspective, what does it look like to accept someone? Does it require agreeing with them on everything they believe and do? Why or why not? Do you believe that people are defined by their sexuality, or is "who they are" more than that?)

No one accepts everything about everyone. For example, you don't accept that Christians reject the morality of certain sexual behaviors, but I don't see that as a harmful rejection of who I am as a person. You simply disagree with my beliefs, just as I disagree with certain LGBTQ beliefs based on what the Bible teaches about God's design for gender and sexuality.

3. Christians are homophobic.

(Questions: What do you mean by homophobic? What examples of Christian homophobia have you seen? Do you believe it's possible to disagree with someone without being motivated by fear?)

To be phobic is to be irrationally fearful of something or someone. Just because Christians believe God has a design for gender and sexuality doesn't mean they have an irrational fear of those who live in other ways.

4. Taking kids to LGBTQ events like pride parades and Drag Queen Story Hour teaches them about diversity and equality. No parent should be opposed to that.

(Questions: What specifically do you think kids should learn about diversity and equality? Is it possible for them to learn those things in contexts other than pride parades and drag queen performances?)

Christians greatly value diversity and equality when rightly defined in terms of God's standards, but culture uses those words to mean something very different (often the moral equality of diverse sexual beliefs and behaviors, which is something I don't agree with as a Christian). My opposition to taking kids to events like pride parades and Drag Queen Story Hour isn't because I don't value teaching kids about diversity and equality, but rather, because I don't believe these events teach kids a *right understanding* of diversity and equality. In addition, these kinds of events often expose young children to highly sexualized content that many people—not only Christians—find age-inappropriate.

5. Book bans are harming LGBTQ kids by removing books from school libraries.

(Questions: Have you personally looked at the books parents are asking to remove? If so, do you share any of their concerns, or do you think

their concerns are completely unfounded? If not, and if you were to find out there's sexually explicit material in them, would you feel differently? Why or why not?)

Most of the books being permanently removed from school libraries have extremely explicit sexual passages or pictures—to the degree that many people consider them pornographic. Just because these books often *also* have LGBTQ themes doesn't automatically mean they're appropriate for kids who identify in that way; *no* kids need access to pornography in their school.

ACTIONS FOR THE COMMON GOOD:
7 Ways to Shine Your Light Through
the Protection of Children

Note that the following ideas shouldn't be seen only as the realm of parents with kids still at home or only as the realm of parents who have their kids in public schools. The common good of children is the realm of all Christians.

1. **Find out about pornographic or otherwise sexualizing books in your local schools and take action accordingly.** The website takebacktheclassroom.com is an example of one organization working to coordinate efforts nationally. You can search for your local school district on the site to see a list of concerning books that have already been found. The organization also has descriptions and images of the books so you can see for yourself what the problems are. They even offer a tool kit that provides a step-by-step guide on how to get problematic books removed from your schools.

2. **Get educated and educate others on the Comprehensive Sexuality Education (CSE) programs being used in schools nationwide.** An excellent, short (56-page), free overview of what CSE programs are and why they're a concern is the Family Research Council's booklet "Sex Education in Public Schools: Sexualization of Children and LGBT Indoctrination."[28] You'll find helpful ideas there for taking action in response to what you learn.

3. **Get educated and educate others on the role of Planned Parenthood in sexualizing children.** Planned Parenthood is (or at least claims to be) the largest provider of sex educa-tion in the US.[29] It's also the nation's largest single provider

of abortions. As sinister as it is, that means they have every financial incentive to encourage sexual activity and experimentation in kids—and they do. Help expose Planned Parenthood's disturbing history and objectives by gathering a group to watch the documentary *The 1916 Project*.[30]

4. **Find out how your local schools are using social emotional learning (SEL).** SEL is a program being used in schools nationwide to supposedly foster social and emotional skills within school curricula. It's wrapped in a lot of positive-sounding language, but many parents don't realize it's thoroughly steeped in critical theory (in particular, critical race theory and queer theory). I highly encourage you to read Lancing and Lindsay's book *The Queering of the American Child* (mentioned earlier in this chapter) to learn more about how this harmless-sounding program gets children to question their identity and reject social norms relating to gender and sexuality. Not every school is using SEL in this way, nor is every teacher. However, these are the philosophical underpinnings of the program, so SEL content and direction in your local schools should be monitored closely. Ask to see lesson plans specifically. If you have concerns about what you find, take them to your school board.[31]

5. **Speak up when organizations hold drag queen events for children.** Graciously express that there are many ways to teach kids important lessons about kindness and diversity other than by bringing in performers who are known in their own community for sexualized performances. Emphasize that even if an organization considers its own event to be a nonsexualized "family-friendly" program, you're one of many people who don't consider *any* drag queen

performance family-friendly given its very nature. Encourage them to consider creating events that appeal to a wider variety of families and don't contribute to the sexualization of children.

6. **Lead the kids or youth at your church in a course on biblical sexuality.** For ages 4-8, I recommend Foundation Worldview's God's Good Design Curriculum.[32] For teens, I recommend Christopher Yuan's 12-lesson series, *The Holy Sexuality Project*.[33] If you're a parent with kids still at home, be sure to start by equipping *them* with this understanding. And if you're involved in a homeschool co-op, consider leading a group there. The more that Christian youth are equipped with a strong understanding of biblical sexuality, the more they'll be prepared to be a light in the world to their peers.

7. **Encourage your pastor to equip your congregation on this issue—and other issues of cultural significance.** It's fitting to make this the last action point in the book because it applies to the subjects of multiple chapters. If your pastor doesn't address issues like these, graciously approach him to ask that he consider doing so. Express your concern for wanting more Christians to be equipped to be salt and light on culturally prominent issues and your desire to see your own church tackle these topics. Pastors have many competing priorities, so don't expect something to happen immediately. But regardless of what your pastor may or may not be willing to do from the pulpit, you can always offer to lead a book study on a culturally important issue yourself (for several ideas, see Recommendations for Further Study beginning on page 237).

LETTING YOUR LIGHT SHINE IN SPITE OF HATE

Take no part in the unfruitful works of darkness, but instead expose them.

EPHESIANS 5:11

■ ■ ■

I'm going to be honest with you. By the time I finished writing this book, I felt the weight of evil in the world more so than ever before.

Writing part 1 was invigorating. These were things I had wanted to say for a long time, and it was exciting to finally put them on paper. I longed to articulate why we need to speak truth even when culture hates us for it; how to think biblically about defining what's truly good for society; why we shouldn't be afraid to get "political" despite the incessant stream of warnings to the contrary from people both in and out of the church. I wanted to equip and inspire—to move Christians to ACT, as I described via this acronym in chapter 5.

But writing part 2 was, frankly, often very dark. I didn't want to write a book that merely explained the biblical view on various hot topics; I wanted to write a book that got inside the head of a culture that loves evil and hates righteousness. That required me to spend months immersed in content produced by culture's dark thinking. I've been following and studying these issues for years from the perspective of a Christian, but you see so much more when you walk in culture's shoes for a while.

The evil becomes palpable in a whole new way.

This is a culture in deep rebellion against its Creator. On *every* topic in part 2, the hatred of Christians ultimately stems from people's deep-seated desire for self-rule. Christian nationalism? Don't impose policies we don't like on us. Secular social justice? Don't impose norms, values, and expectations on us. Abortion? Don't impose bodily rules on us. Transgenderism? Don't impose gender restrictions on us. Sexuality? Don't impose sexual restrictions on us.

Ultimately, it's not Christians that culture hates.

It's God.

We're just His messengers.

As I said in chapter 1, righteousness is despised by a fallen world. Consequently, when God's messengers advocate for righteousness in society, it means we're working for people's good *against their own desires*. They may want to go their own way, but when we know God's way is the only good way, we have to be willing to shine our light in the darkness even when people hate us for it.

Feeling the weight of evil in the world has given me a fresh appreciation for how desperately that light is needed. Yes, evil is dark, but exposing the unfruitful works of darkness puts God's goodness on beautiful display for the world to see (Ephesians 5:11). It points people to the glory of God…if they're willing to look. We're not responsible for *making* them look, but we are responsible for lighting the way.

Lest anyone feel overly weighed down by the darkness of the world, always remember that when Jesus comes again, all sin and suffering will be destroyed. All wrongs will be made right. As the Bible says, "We are waiting for new heavens and a new earth in which righteousness dwells" (2 Peter 3:13).

I can't wait for righteousness to dwell.

In the meantime, may we all persevere as Christians in a hostile public square for the glory of God and the good of others.

RECOMMENDATIONS FOR FURTHER STUDY

■ ■ ■

As an avid reader, it's a terrifying prospect to choose books for a recommended resource list. There are far more excellent books than I can include here! That said, my goal with this list is to provide recommendations that I've found especially helpful and to offer several options to choose from depending on a person's varied levels of background knowledge and interest.

Books within the subject categories below are listed in alphabetical order by author, not by strength of recommendation. Note that my recommendation of these books doesn't necessarily imply I agree with every statement made within them—only that I recommend them as valuable resources on the subjects listed.

How We Got to Our Cultural Moment

- Erwin Lutzer, *The Eclipse of God: Our Nation's Disastrous Search for a More Inclusive Deity (and What We Must Do About It)* (Eugene, OR: Harvest House Publishers, 2024).

- Carl Trueman, *The Rise and Triumph of the Modern Self: Cultural Amnesia, Expressive Individualism, and the Road to Sexual Revolution* (Wheaton, IL: Crossway, 2020).

Understanding and Responding to Culture from a Biblical Worldview

- Natasha Crain, *Faithfully Different: Regaining Biblical Clarity in a Secular Culture* (Eugene, OR: Harvest House Publishers, 2022).

- Jack Hibbs, *Living in the Daze of Deception* (Eugene, OR: Harvest House Publishers, 2024).

- Gregory Koukl, *Street Smarts: Using Questions to Answer Christianity's Toughest Challenges* (Grand Rapids, MI: Zondervan, 2023).

- Gregory Koukl, *Tactics: A Game Plan for Discussing Your Christian Convictions,* 10th Anniversary Edition (Grand Rapids, MI: Zondervan, 2019).

- Erwin Lutzer, *We Will Not Be Silenced: Responding Courageously to Our Culture's Assault on Christianity* (Eugene, OR: Harvest House Publishers, 2020).

- Aaron Renn, *Life in the Negative World: Confronting Challenges in an Anti-Christian Culture* (Grand Rapids, MI: Zondervan, 2024).

Christian Political History and Engagement

- Greg Forster, *The Contested Public Square: The Crisis of Christianity and Politics* (Westmont, IL: IVP Academic, 2008).

- Frank Turek and Norman Geisler, *Legislating Morality: Is It Wise? Is It Legal? Is It Possible?* (Eugene, OR: Wipf and Stock Publishers, 2023).

Christian Nationalism

- Mark David Hall, *Did America Have a Christian Founding?: Separating Modern Myth from Historical Truth* (Nashville, TN: Thomas Nelson, 2019).

- Mark David Hall, *Who's Afraid of Christian Nationalism?: Why Christian Nationalism Is Not an Existential Threat to America or the Church* (Nashville, TN: Fidelis Books, 2024).

Secular Social Justice and Biblical Justice

- Voddie T. Baucham Jr., *Fault Lines: The Social Justice Movement and Evangelicalism's Looming Catastrophe* (Washington, DC: Salem Books, 2021).

- Voddie T. Baucham Jr., *It's Not Like Being Black: How Sexual Activists Hijacked the Civil Rights Movement* (Washington, DC: Regnery Faith, 2024).

- Krista Bontrager and Monique Duson, *Walking in Unity: Biblical Answers to Questions on Race and Racism* (Eugene, OR: Harvest House Publishers, 2024).

- Logan Lancing and James Lindsay, *The Queering of the American Child: How a New School Religious Cult Poisons the Minds and Bodies of Normal Kids* (Orlando, FL: New Discourses, 2024). *Not written from a Christian perspective.

- Helen Pluckrose and James Lindsay, *Cynical Theories: How Activist Scholarship Made Everything about Race, Gender, and Identity—and Why This Harms Everybody* (Durham, NC: Pitchstone Publishing, 2020). *Not written from a Christian perspective.

- Neil Shenvi and Pat Sawyer, *Critical Dilemma: The Rise of Critical Theories and Social Justice Ideology—Implications for the Church and Society* (Eugene, OR: Harvest House Publishers, 2023).

- Thaddeus Williams, *Confronting Injustice Without Compromising Truth: 12 Questions Christians Should Ask About Social Justice* (Grand Rapids, MI: Zondervan Academic, 2020).

Abortion

- Ryan T. Anderson and Alexandra DeSanctis, *How Abortion Harms Everything and Solves Nothing* (Washington, DC: Regnery Publishing, 2022).

- Seth Gruber, *The 1916 Project: The Lyin', the Witch, and the War We're In* (Ottawa, KS: Vindex Media, 2024).

- Scott Klusendorf, *The Case for Life: Equipping Christians to Engage the Culture*, second edition (Wheaton, IL: Crossway, 2023).

- Marvin Olasky and Leah Savas, *The Story of Abortion in America: A Street-Level History, 1652–2022* (Wheaton, IL: Crossway, 2022).

Gender and Sexuality

- Rosaria Butterfield, *Five Lies of Our Anti-Christian Age* (Wheaton, IL: Crossway, 2023).

- Becket Cook, *A Change of Affection: A Gay Man's Incredible Story of Redemption* (Nashville, TN: Thomas Nelson, 2019).

- Nancy Pearcey, *Love Thy Body: Answering Hard Questions about Life and Sexuality* (Grand Rapids, MI: Baker Books, 2018).

- Laura Perry, *Transgender to Transformed: A Story of Transition That Will Truly Set You Free* (Tulsa, OK: Genesis Publishing Group, 2019).

- Abigail Shrier, *Irreversible Damage: The Transgender Craze Seducing Our Daughters* (Washington, DC: Regnery Publishing, 2021).

- Frank Turek, *Correct, Not Politically Correct: About Same-Sex Marriage and Transgenderism*, expanded third edition (CrossExamined.org, 2023).

- Andrew T. Walker, *God and the Transgender Debate: What Does the Bible Actually Say About Gender Identity?* (Charlotte, NC: The Good Book Company, 2017).

- Christopher Yuan and Angela Yuan, *Out of a Far Country: A Gay Son's Journey to God. A Broken Mother's Search for Hope* (Colorado Springs, CO: WaterBrook, 2011).

NOTES

■ ■ ■

Chapter 1—Jesus Said It Would Happen

1. My analyses in this book are focused on what Christians in the United States are experiencing, but Christians in other Western countries are certainly experiencing much of the same. Thus, while this book is primarily for an American audience given the specifics I'll discuss, I do hope it will benefit Christians in other countries who are experiencing similar cultural hostilities.

Chapter 2—God Defines the Common Good

1. This succinct definition was articulated by Christian ethics professor Andrew T. Walker in his article "What Is the 'Common Good'?," *Crossway*, https://www.crossway.org/articles/what-is-the-common-good/.

2. Because this book is intended for Christians who have a biblical worldview—or at least *want* to have a biblical worldview—I'm not going to make a case for biblical authority here. For those who need more background on why there's good reason to believe the Bible is the authoritative Word of God, I recommend starting with J. Warner Wallace's *Cold Case Christianity: A Homicide Detective Investigates the Claims of the Gospels,* updated and expanded edition (Colorado Springs, CO: David C. Cook, 2023). For those looking for a more in-depth resource, I recommend Craig Blomberg's *The Historical Reliability of the New Testament: Countering the Challenges to Evangelical Christian Beliefs* (Nashville, TN: B&H Academic, 2016).

3. Jeffrey M. Jones, "Belief in God in U.S. Dips to 81%, a New Low," *Gallup*, June 17, 2022, https://news.gallup.com/poll/393737/belief-god-dips-new-low.aspx.

4. Progressive Christians may consider themselves Bible-believing because they accept certain truths taught in Scripture, but I use the term here to delineate between those who accept the full Bible as God's authoritative truth and those who do not.

5. J. Budziszewski, *What We Can't Not Know* (revised and expanded edition) (San Francisco, CA: Ignatius Press, 2011), 222, 228.

6. Stated during Robert Sirico's talk "The Free & Virtuous Society," *YouTube*, March 29, 2023, https://www.youtube.com/watch?v=vkWrrK55BDY.

7. "American Worldview Inventory 2021, Release #5: Top 10 Most Seductive Unbiblical Ideas Embraced by Americans," *Arizona Christian University*, PDF download, https://www.arizonachristian.edu/wp-content/uploads/2021/06/CRC_AWVI2021_Release05_Digital_01_20210618.pdf.

Chapter 3—When the Common Good Is Political

1. "Politics," *Wikipedia*, https://simple.wikipedia.org/wiki/Politics.

2. An excellent overview of much of this history is George Athas's *Bridging the Testaments: The History and Theology of God's People in the Second Temple Period* (Grand Rapids, MI: Zondervan, 2023).

3. For those interested in a detailed treatment of the subject, I recommend Greg Forster's *The Contested Public Square: The Crisis of Christianity and Politics* (Downers Grove, IL: IVP Academic, 2008).

4. Forster, *The Contested Public Square*, 147.

5. We'll talk more about this in chapter 6, but for a great overview on this subject, I recommend Mark David Hall's *Did America Have a Christian Founding?: Separating Modern Myth from Historical Truth* (Nashville, TN: Thomas Nelson, 2020).

6. Natasha Crain, *Faithfully Different: Regaining Biblical Clarity in a Secular Culture* (Eugene, OR: Harvest House Publishers, 2022), 29.

7. I discuss these statistics and many more in detail in *Faithfully Different*. At the time I wrote *Faithfully Different*, the percentage of people with a biblical worldview was reported to be 6 percent. I have updated the number here to 4 percent to reflect the latest American Worldview Inventory results (2023), which can be found here: "American Worldview Inventory 2023, Release #1: Incidence of Biblical Worldview Shows Significant Change Since the Start of the Pandemic," *Arizona Christian University*, PDF download, https://www.arizonachristian.edu/wp-content/uploads/2023/02/CRC_AWVI2023_Release1.pdf.

8. See, for example, this article: Lily Sanchez, "Why We Should Abolish the Family," *Current Affairs*, September 5, 2022, https://www.currentaffairs.org/2022/09/why-we-should-abolish-the-family.

Chapter 4—Should Christians Impose Their Views on Others?

1. Some of you may be well-versed in ideas such as sphere sovereignty and two kingdom theology and have self-selected into reading this endnote given your surprise that I would say most people aren't debating the finer points of political theology. If you happen to be someone who is, that's great! But please note I said the *typical* objection is not of this nature.

2. It's worth noting, however, that the Founding Fathers worked from theistic (if not always specifically Christian) assumptions. The Declaration of Independence, for example, asserts a natural law theism and corresponding God-given rights. So, while the United States was not founded upon the authority of a specific religion, that doesn't mean there were no worldview assumptions on the part of the founders.

3. Betsy Cooper, Daniel Cox, Rachel Lienesch, and Robert P. Jones, "Exodus: Why Americans are Leaving Religion—and Why They're Unlikely to Come Back," *PRRI*, September 22, 2016, https://www.prri.org/research/prri-rns-poll-nones-atheist-leaving-religion/.

4. Nicholas Kristof, "Progressive Christians Arise! Hallelujah!," *The New York Times*, March 20, 2021, https://www.nytimes.com/2021/03/20/opinion/sunday/progressive-christians-politics.html. I responded to his article here: "No, The Growth of Progressive Christian Politicians is Not a Good Thing for America," *Natasha Crain*, March 22, 2021, https://natashacrain.com/no-the-growth-of-progressive-christian-politicians-is-not-a-good-thing-for-america-a-response-to-the-new-york-times-opinion-piece-by-nicholas-kristof/.

5. Andy Stanley, *Not in It to Win It: Why Choosing Sides Sidelines the Church* (Grand Rapids, MI: Zondervan, 2022), 32.

6. "Party Affiliation," *Pew Research Center*, https://www.pewresearch.org/religion/religious-landscape-study/party-affiliation/.

Chapter 5—Persevering in the Public Square

1. See the following PDF for more information on methodology: "American Worldview Inventory Methodology," *Arizona Christian University*, PDF download, https://www.arizonachristian.edu/wp-content/uploads/2022/06/AWVI-2021-22-Methodology-Brief_Digital.pdf. Additionally, I interviewed Dr. Barna on my podcast regarding further detail. That interview can be found here: "What Is a Biblical Worldview? with George Barna," *Natasha Crain*, September 12, 2022, https://natashacrain.com/what-is-a-biblical-worldview-with-george-barna/.

2. I recommend starting with J. Warner Wallace's *Cold Case Christianity: A Homicide Detective Investigates the Claims of the Gospels*, updated and expanded edition (Colorado Springs, CO: David C. Cook, 2023). For those looking for a more in-depth resource, I recommend Craig Blomberg's *The Historical Reliability of the New Testament: Countering the Challenges to Evangelical Christian Beliefs* (Nashville, TN: B&H Academic, 2016).

3. Lest anyone mischaracterize what I'm saying, I'm not suggesting that the Bible dropped out of the sky. The Bible contains 66 books written by 40-plus authors over 1,600 years. Today we have a "book"—the end product of God working through multiple authors over many years—and that's what I'm referring to here.

4. Sue Briner and Kai Ryan, "Christians compelled to advocate for best transgender care," *Beaumont Enterprise*, March 30, 2023, https://www.beaumontenterprise.com/opinions/columns/article/christians-compelled-advocate-best-transgender-17863347.php.

5. Natasha Crain, *Faithfully Different: Regaining Biblical Clarity in a Secular Culture* (Eugene, OR: Harvest House Publishers, 2022).

6. Aaron Renn, "The Three Worlds of Evangelicalism," *First Things*, February 2022, https://www.firstthings.com/article/2022/02/the-three-worlds-of-evangelicalism.

7. Aaron Renn, *Life in the Negative World: Confronting Challenges in an Anti-Christian Culture* (Grand Rapids, MI: Zondervan Reflective, 2024), 34.

8. Aside from mindset changes, Renn's book also addresses several practical ways Christians can prepare for financial risk. I recommend reading his book and considering what that may look like in your own situation.

Chapter 6—Dangerous Christian Nationalists

1. In order to avoid redundancy, I'll refer to the mainstream media simply as "the media" in the body of this chapter. In doing so, I'm not claiming *all* media are promoting the views we'll discuss here, but rather, the majority of traditional, established mass media outlets.

2. Ja'han Jones, "Christian nationalists are a small and dangerous group with outsized power," *MSNBC.com*, February 29, 2024, https://www.msnbc.com/the-reidout/reidout-blog/christian-nationalists-republicans-rcna141239.

3. "Support for Christian Nationalism in All 50 States: Findings from PRRI's 2023 American Values Atlas," *PRRI*, February 28, 2024, https://www.prri.org/research/support-for-christian-nationalism-in-all-50-states/.

4. Katherine Stewart, "Christian Nationalists Are Excited About What Comes Next," *The New York Times*, July 5, 2022, https://www.nytimes.com/2022/07/05/opinion/dobbs-christian-nationalism.html.

5. "Christianity's place in politics, and 'Christian nationalism,'" *Pew Research Center*, March 15, 2024, https://www.pewresearch.org/religion/2024/03/15/christianitys-place-in-politics-and-christian-nationalism/.

6. Andrew L. Whitehead and Samuel L. Perry, *Taking America Back for God: Christian Nationalism in the United States* (New York: Oxford University Press, 2022), 14.

7. Because this book is focused on how culture views Christians, theological concerns from *within* the church about ideas sometimes labeled *Christian nationalism* are intentionally left out of this chapter's discussion given space considerations (for example, belief that America is a chosen nation or that Christians have a "Seven Mountain Mandate" to bring change to the seven major spheres of influence in society). Belief in a Seven Mountain Mandate is especially associated with the New Apostolic Reformation (NAR), a movement that promotes a host of unbiblical ideas. For those interested in learning more about NAR, I highly recommend Holly Pivec and Douglas Geivett's book *Counterfeit Kingdom: The Dangers of New Revelation, New Prophets, and New Age Practices in the Church* (Nashville, TN: B&H Books, 2022).

8. Whitehead and Perry, *Taking America Back for God*, 165.

9. Whitehead and Perry, *Taking America Back for God*, viii.

10. Whitehead and Perry, *Taking America Back for God*, 7.

11. Whitehead and Perry, *Taking America Back for God*, 26. Whitehead and Perry acknowledge that to some degree they consider both of these groups "Christian nationalists," not just the Ambassadors.

12. Whitehead and Perry, *Taking America Back for God*, 16.

13. Whitehead and Perry, *Taking America Back for God*, 83.

14. "Support for Christian Nationalism in All 50 States."

15. "Support for Christian Nationalism in All 50 States."

16. In a constitutional federal republic, the power is vested in the people as in a democracy, but the constitution dictates boundaries of that power in order to protect individual rights.

17. Mark David Hall, "Theology of Politics | Christian Nationalism," *Standing for Freedom Center*, February 8, 2022, https://www.standingforfreedom.com/white-paper/tilting-at-windmills-the-threat-of-christian-nationalism/.

18. Adam Gabbatt, "US set for flurry of 'Christian nationalist' bills advanced by religious right," *The Guardian*, January 15, 2021, https://www.theguardian.com/world/2021/jan/15/christian-nationalist-religious-right-legislation-bills.

19. Oren Oppenheim, "'Christian nationalism' threatens democracy, some experts say," *ABC News*, November 7, 2022, https://abcnews.go.com/Politics/christian-nationalism-threatens-democracy-experts/story?id=91866475.

20. "Politico reporter goes viral with comments on 'Christian nationalists,'" *Fox News*, February 23, 2024, https://www.foxnews.com/video/6347475500112. Note that after much criticism, Przybyla attempted to clarify her comments, but in effect doubled down on the same claim. See https://twitter.com/HeidiReports/status/1761064510561861962.

21. Whitehead and Perry also discuss the "racially intolerant attitudes" of their Christian nationalist respondents, but because their discussion casts a much wider net of what they consider racism, I'm limiting my discussion here to the PRRI study in the interest of space. Similar points could be made, however, from Whitehead and Perry's approach.

22. "A Christian Nation? Understanding the Threat of Christian Nationalism to American

Democracy and Culture," *PRRI*, February 8, 2023, https://www.prri.org/research/a-christian
-nation-understanding-the-threat-of-christian-nationalism-to-american-democracy-and-culture/.

23. "A Christian Nation? Understanding the Threat of Christian Nationalism to American Democracy and Culture."

24. Whitehead and Perry, *Taking America Back for God*, 92.

25. "A Christian Nation? Understanding the Threat of Christian Nationalism to American Democracy and Culture."

26. "How Americans View the Situation at the U.S.-Mexico Border, Its Causes and Consequences," *Pew Research Center*, February 15, 2024, https://www.pewresearch.org/politics/2024/02/15/how-americans-view-the-situation-at-the-u-s-mexico-border-its-causes-and-consequences/.

27. *Congress.gov*, https://www.congress.gov/members/find-your-member.

Chapter 7—Power-Hungry Oppressors

1. "The Statement on Social Justice & the Gospel," *SJ&G*, https://statementonsocialjustice.com/.

2. John Pavlovitz, "Jesus Was a Social Justice Warrior," September 15, 2018, https://johnpavlovitz.com/2018/09/15/the-real-statement-on-social-justice-the-gospel/.

3. Ironically, Pavlovitz identifies as a progressive Christian, but as we saw previously, progressive Christians tend to hold the same moral views as secular culture does. This is especially the case on social justice issues. The thinking represented in the excerpt I quoted mirrors secular social justice thinking precisely.

4. "If there are gods, why is the world so full of pain and injustice?," *Quora.com*, https://www.quora.com/If-there-are-gods-why-is-the-world-so-full-of-pain-and-injustice.

5. Özlem Sensoy and Robin DiAngelo, *Is Everyone Really Equal?: An Introduction to Key Concepts in Social Justice* (New York: Teachers College Press, 2017), 61.

6. Marina Watts, "In Smithsonian Race Guidelines, Rational Thinking and Hard Work Are White Values," *Newsweek*, updated May 25, 2021, https://www.newsweek.com/smithsonian-race-guidelines-rational-thinking-hard-work-are-white-values-1518333.

7. "The Nuclear Family is a System of Oppression? Thomas Sowell," *YouTube*, https://www.youtube.com/watch?v=Ly0I9WQTV-4.

8. It's worth noting that there are other reasons for the association of whiteness and Christianity as well—especially the history of European colonialism. For purposes of my points here, I'm only highlighting this specific factor.

9. David Halperin, *Saint Foucault: Towards a Gay Hagiography* (New York: Oxford University Press, 1995), 62.

10. Christopher Rufo, a Senior Fellow at the Manhattan Institute, has documented much of this through his investigative work. Readers can review examples here: "A Parent's Guide to Radical Gender Theory," February 9, 2023, https://christopherrufo.com/p/a-parents-guide-to-radical-gender-theory and "Soldiers for the Gender Revolution," August 10, 2022, www.city-journal.org/article/soldiers-for-the-gender-revolution.

11. For an extended discussion of this claim, see Greg Koukl's excellent article "The Legend of the Social Justice Jesus," *Stand to Reason*, https://www.str.org/w/the-legend-of-the-social-justice-jesus.

12. "About Human Trafficking," *US Department of State*, https://www.state.gov/human trafficking-about-human-trafficking/.

13. "World Watch List 2024," *Open Doors*, https://www.opendoors.org/en-US/persecution/countries/.

14. "The AFCARS Report," *U.S. Department of Health and Human Services*, June 28, 2022, PDF download, https://www.acf.hhs.gov/sites/default/files/documents/cb/afcars-report-29.pdf.

15. *Safe Families for Children,* https://safe-families.org/.

Chapter 8—Controlling Misogynists

1. The right to abortion was granted without restriction during the first trimester. Individual states could choose to impose *some* restrictions during the second trimester and ban abortion during the third.

2. "Dobbs v. Jackson Women's Health Organization," *US Supreme Court*, June 24, 2022, PDF download, https://www.supremecourt.gov/opinions/21pdf/19-1392_6j37.pdf, 201-202.

3. Ibid., 149.

4. Linda Greenhouse, "Religious Doctrine, Not the Constitution, Drove the Dobbs Decision," *The New York Times*, July 22, 2022, https://www.nytimes.com/2022/07/22/opinion/abortion-religion-supreme-court.html.

5. Alex Morris, "Think Christianity Is Anti-Abortion? Think Again," *Rolling Stone*, June 27, 2022, https://www.rollingstone.com/politics/political-commentary/think-christianity-is-anti-abortion-think-again-1374697/.

6. "Roe v. Wade," *US Supreme Court*, January 22, 1973, PDF download, https://tile.loc.gov/storage-services/service/ll/usrep/usrep410/usrep410113/usrep410113.pdf.

7. "Fourteenth Amendment Equal Protection and Other Rights," *Constitution Annotated*, https://constitution.congress.gov/browse/amendment-14/.

8. "Dobbs v. Jackson Women's Health Organization," 14.

9. "Dobbs v. Jackson Women's Health Organization," 13.

10. "Dobbs v. Jackson Women's Health Organization," 77.

11. "Declaration of Independence: A Transcription," *National Archives*, https://www.archives.gov/founding-docs/declaration-transcript.

12. "Views about abortion," *Pew Research Center*, https://www.pewresearch.org/religious-landscape-study/database/views-about-abortion/.

13. "Roe v Wade topic came up in (Christian) church," *Reddit*, https://www.reddit.com/r/TwoXChromosomes/comments/vl6034/roe_v_wade_topic_came_up_in_christian_church/.

14. It's sometimes argued that Exodus 21:22-23 is biblical evidence that preborn babies have less value than other human beings, but this is based on a faulty understanding of the passage. For a helpful explanation of how these verses actually show the reverse—that preborn babies have *as much* value as other humans—see the following article: Tim Chaffey, "Does the Bible Condone Abortion?," *Answers in Genesis*, https://answersingenesis.org/sanctity-of-life/abortion/does-the-bible-condone-abortion/.

15. Quoted in Scott Klusendorf, *The Case for Life: Equipping Christians to Engage the Culture*, second edition (Wheaton, IL: Crossway, 2023), 55. The textbook is titled *The Developing Human: Clinically Oriented Embryology*.

16. Stephen D. Schwartz, *The Moral Question of Abortion* (Chicago, IL: Loyola University Press, 1990), 15-17.

17. Scott Klusendorf, "Speaking Up to Defend Life," *Focus on the Family*, https://www.focusonthefamily.com/pro-life/speaking-up-to-defend-life/.

18. We could also make the case with more space that knowledge of the value of human life is part of general revelation, as discussed in chapter 2. I'm saying "from the Bible" here only because that's what we addressed in this chapter.

19. In case anyone is wondering, that also means it's not a God-given right. Because the Bible clearly condemns the unjustified taking of innocent human life, that necessarily implies it's not a right to which God entitles people.

20. Posted to X here: https://twitter.com/CollinRugg/status/1779142096773157184.

21. "Dobbs v. Jackson Women's Health Organization," 149.

22. Mary E. Harned and Ingrid Skop, "Pro-Life Laws Protect Mom and Baby: Pregnant Women's Lives are Protected in All States," *Charlotte Lozier Institute*, September 11, 2023, https://lozierinstitute .org/pro-life-laws-protect-mom-and-baby-pregnant-womens-lives-are-protected-in-all-states/.

23. Christina Francis, "Ectopic Pregnancy and Abortion," *Focus on the Family*, January 13, 2023, https://www.focusonthefamily.com/pro-life/ectopic-pregnancy-and-abortion/.

Chapter 9–Cruel Rights-Deniers

1. Jamie Bruesehoff, "My Transgender Daughter is a Beloved Child of God," *Medium*, March 1, 2017, https://medium.com/@jamiebruesehoff/my-transgender-daughter-is-a-beloved-child-of -god-52a92a89f6e4.This story was also shared at the *HuffPost* on March 7, 2017: https://www .huffpost.com/entry/my-transgender-daughter-is-a-beloved-child-of-god_b_58bedb5fe4b0d 8c45f46c3de.

2. There is disagreement among Christians over whether we should use pronouns that reflect transgender people's biological sex or pronouns they choose for themselves. It's my conviction that we should use pronouns that align with biological sex to avoid any appearance of support- ing the false idea that men can actually become women and women can actually become men. Rebekah's mom refers to her child as a girl with female pronouns, but I refer to him here as a boy based on his biological sex. This is not out of disrespect (as some might see it), but rather, out of respect for Rebekah's God-given biological design—something we'll discuss the impor- tance of in this chapter.

3. "20:20 My Secret Self Complete Documentary," *YouTube*, https://www.youtube.com/ watch?v=eJ_BHY5RolA.

4. My use of the term *transgender* in this chapter is not to suggest that anyone can actually change their gender, but rather, to avoid having to repeatedly use the more cumbersome term *trans- gender-identifying person*.

5. Caroline Framke, "How Jazz Jennings Changed the World for Trans Youth Simply by Being Herself," *Variety*, June 2, 2021, https://variety.com/2021/tv/features/jazz-jennings-i-am-jazz -trans-legislation-1234985248/.

6. 579 represents the number of bills considered "anti-trans" by transgender activists and are doc- umented here: *Trans Legislation Tracker*, https://translegislation.com/. There are bills that have the opposite intended effect—to *support* transgender ideology—in other states, but those have not (to my knowledge) been quantified in the same way at the time of this writing.

7. Rachel Minkin and Anna Brown, "Rising shares of U.S. adults know someone who is trans- gender or goes by gender-neutral pronouns," *Pew Research Center*, July 27, 2021, https://www .pewresearch.org/short-reads/2021/07/27/rising-shares-of-u-s-adults-know-someone-who-is -transgender-or-goes-by-gender-neutral-pronouns/.

8. Josh Olds, "Raising Kids Beyond the Binary | A Conversation with Jamie Bruesehoff,"

Life Is Story, February 29, 2024, https://www.lifeisstory.com/podcast/raising-kids-beyond-the-binary-a-conversation-with-jamie-bruesehoff/.

9. *Diagnostic and Statistical Manual of Mental Disorders: DSM-III* (Washington, DC: American Psychiatric Association, 1980), 261-262.

10. *Diagnostic and Statistical Manual of Mental Disorders: DSM-5* (Washington, DC: American Psychiatric Association, 2013).

11. "A Guide for Working With Transgender and Gender Nonconforming Patients," *American Psychiatric Association*, https://www.psychiatry.org/psychiatrists/diversity/education/transgender-and-gender-nonconforming-patients/gender-dysphoria-diagnosis.

12. "Frequently Asked Questions about Transgender People," *National Center for Transgender Equality*, July 9, 2016, https://transequality.org/issues/resources/frequently-asked-questions-about-transgender-people.

13. Anna Brown, "About 5% of young adults in the U.S. say their gender is different from their sex assigned at birth," *Pew Research Center*, June 7, 2022, https://www.pewresearch.org/short-reads/2022/06/07/about-5-of-young-adults-in-the-u-s-say-their-gender-is-different-from-their-sex-assigned-at-birth/.

14. Estimates of people identifying as transgender vary across sources based on the data collection methodology. For an in-depth look at other estimates, see "How Many Adults and Youth Identify as Transgender in the United States?," *UCLA School of Law Williams Institute*, PDF download, https://williamsinstitute.law.ucla.edu/wp-content/uploads/Trans-Pop-Update-Jun-2022.pdf.

15. Per the prior endnote, estimates vary, but sources consistently show that biological females account for nearly half, if not more, of transgender-identifying people.

16. Abigail Shrier, *Irreversible Damage: The Transgender Craze Seducing Our Daughters* (Washington, DC: Regnery Publishing, 2020).

17. Shrier, *Irreversible Damage*, 25.

18. Shrier, *Irreversible Damage*, XXVI.

19. Shrier, *Irreversible Damage*, 26.

20. Shrier, *Irreversible Damage*, 28.

21. Shrier, *Irreversible Damage*, 28.

22. Helena Kirschner, "By Any Other Name," *Substack*, February 19, 2022, https://lacroicsz.substack.com/p/by-any-other-name.

23. Kirschner, "By Any Other Name."

24. If you're interested in more deeply understanding the thought process that has led and is leading so many teen girls into transgender ideology, I recommend reading Kirschner's detailed account.

25. An insightful interview with another detransitioner is Jordan Peterson's interview with Chloe Cole: "The Wounds That Won't Heal | Detransitioner Chloe Cole | EP 319," *YouTube*, https://www.youtube.com/watch?v=6O3MzPeomqs.

26. "How Many Adults and Youth Identify as Transgender in the United States?," *UCLA School of Law Williams Institute*.

27. See, for example, this in-depth report from Reuters: "A Reuters Special Report: As more transgender children seek medical care, families confront many unknowns," *Reuters*, October 6, 2022, https://www.reuters.com/investigates/special-report/usa-transyouth-care/.

28. Andrew T. Walker, *God and the Transgender Debate: What Does the Bible Actually Say About Gender Identity?* (Charlotte, NC: The Good Book Company, 2017), 53.

29. "Gender Discomfort and Autism," *Autism Research Institute*, https://autism.org/gender-discomfort-and-autism/.

30. "Tracking the rise of anti-trans bills in the U.S.," *Trans Legislation Tracker*, https://translegislation.com/learn.

31. "Tracking the rise of anti-trans bills in the U.S."

32. Lindsey Dawson and Anna Rouw, "Half of All U.S. States Limit or Prohibit Youth Access to Gender Affirming Care," *KFF*, May 29, 2024, https://www.kff.org/other/issue-brief/half-of-all-u-s-states-limit-or-prohibit-youth-access-to-gender-affirming-care.

33. To learn more about how to impact your public schools through your school board and other methods, listen to my two-part interview with Andy White on *The Natasha Crain Podcast*: "34. Public Schools: What Christian Parents Need to Know" and "35. Public Schools (Part 2): How to Know What's Going On in the Classroom," https://natashacrain.com/podcast/.

34. For more information on these cases, listen to my podcast interview with Ryan Bangert from Alliance Defending Freedom: "The State of Parental Rights, with Ryan Bangert of Alliance Defending Freedom," https://natashacrain.com/the-state-of-parental-rights-with-ryan-bangert-of-alliance-defending-freedom/.

35. "A Response to an Employer's Request for Pronouns," *Stand to Reason*, https://www.str.org/w/a-response-to-an-employer-s-request-for-pronouns.

36. Laura Perry, *Transgender to Transformed: A Story of Transition That Will Truly Set You Free* (Tulsa, OK: Genesis Publishing Group, 2019).

Chapter 10—Hateful Bigots

1. Madsen wrote under the pen name Erastes Pill. Marshall Kirk and Erastes Pill, "The Overhauling of Straight America," *Guide Magazine*, November 1987, http://library.gayhomeland.org/0018/EN/EN_Overhauling_Straight.htm.

2. Marshall Kirk and Hunter Madsen, *After the Ball: How America Will Conquer Its Fear and Hatred of Gays in the 90's* (New York: Plume, 1990).

3. See this article as one example: Mey Rude, "Target Is Removing Some Pride Merch Because Bigots Complained," *Out*, May 24, 2023, https://www.out.com/news/target-pride-collection.

4. Sigmund Freud, *Civilization and Its Discontents*, trans. James Strachey (New York: W.W. Norton, 1989), 56.

5. I say "most" because even Freud recognized that there were at least *some* necessary restrictions on sex drive in order to make civilization possible. However, he saw traditional sexual morality as far *too* restrictive.

6. Kinsey Institute, https://kinseyinstitute.org/research/publications/kinsey-scale.php.

7. Alfred Kinsey, *Sexual Behavior in the Human Male* (Philadelphia, PA: W.B. Saunders Company, 1949), 585, 597, 650. Accessed online at https://archive.org/details/in.ernet.dli.2015.187552/mode/2up.

8. Kinsey, *Sexual Behavior in the Human Male*, 203.

9. Kinsey, *Sexual Behavior in the Human Male*, 176-177.

10. Kinsey, *Sexual Behavior in the Human Male*, 176.

11. Kinsey, *Sexual Behavior in the Human Male*, 180.

12. Kinsey, *Sexual Behavior in the Human Male*, 181.

13. Kinsey, *Sexual Behavior in the Human Female* (Philadelphia, PA: W.B. Saunders Company, 1953), 121. Accessed online at https://archive.org/details/sexualbehaviorin00inst/page/n5/mode/2up.

14. Gayle S. Rubin, "Thinking Sex: Notes for a Radical Theory of the Politics of Sexuality," 1984, available online at https://bpb-us-e2.wpmucdn.com/sites.middlebury.edu/dist/2/3378/files/2015/01/Rubin-Thinking-Sex.pdf.

15. Hannah Dyer, "Queer futurity and childhood innocence: Beyond the injury of development," *Global Studies of Childhood*, 7(3), 290-302, https://journals.sagepub.com/doi/full/10.1177/2043610616671056.

16. Dyer, "Queer futurity and childhood innocence."

17. The organization dropped "Queen" from the name in October 2022 and is now referred to as Drag Story Hour (DSH). I use this most recent acronym in the chapter for consistency, though it wasn't technically used prior to 2022.

18. You can read how one drag queen performer describes DSH here: Veranda L'Ni as Told to Elizabeth Yuko, "I'm a Drag Queen—Here's What Really Happens at a Drag Queen Story Hour," June 6, 2023, https://www.rd.com/article/drag-queen-story-hour/.

19. Wendy Robinson, "TikTok Mom Goes Undercover To Reveal the Kind of 'Trauma' Kids Endure at a Drag Brunch," *CafeMom*, March 13, 2023, https://cafemom.com/parenting/tiktok-mom-takes-kids-to-drag-brunch-trauma.

20. All of the following quotes are from Harper Keenan and Lil Miss Hot Mess, "Drag Pedagogy: The Playful Practice of Queer Imagination in Early Childhood," *Curriculum Inquiry*, 50(5), 440–61, https://www.tandfonline.com/doi/full/10.1080/03626784.2020.1864621.

21. Logan Lancing with James Lindsay, *The Queering of the American Child: How a New School Religious Cult Poisons the Minds and Bodies of Normal Kids* (Orlando, FL: New Discourses, 2024).

22. The following article provides helpful statistics and a brief overview of the kinds of books being "banned": Max Eden, "Parents Objecting to Pornographic Material in School Libraries Aren't 'Book Banners,'" *Heritage Foundation*, October 6, 2023, https://www.heritage.org/education/commentary/parents-objecting-pornographic-material-school-libraries-arent-book-banners.

23. Kristine Parks, "'Family-friendly' Pride parade in West Hollywood had men depicting graphic BDSM sexual act," *Fox News*, June 5, 2023, https://www.foxnews.com/media/family-friendly-pride-parade-west-hollywood-men-depicting-graphic-bdsm-sexual-act.

24. I'm not suggesting that every person embracing the sexual revolution would necessarily identify themselves as an atheist or deist, but rather, that the claims of the sexual revolution are the logical outworking of an atheistic or deistic view. Many people have never thought through the worldview assumptions underpinning their beliefs.

25. "Queer Planet | Official Trailer | Peacock Original," *YouTube*, https://www.youtube.com/watch?v=GikfSszcBHE.

26. Kevin DeYoung, *What Does the Bible Really Teach about Homosexuality?* (Wheaton, IL: Crossway, 2015).

27. The organization Gays Against Groomers is one example: https://www.gaysagainstgroomers.com/.

28. Cathy Ruse, "Sex Education in Public Schools: Sexualization of Children and LGBT Indoctrination," *Family Research Council*, https://www.frc.org/brochure/sex-education-in-public-schools-sexualization-of-children-and-lgbt-indoctrination.

29. "Sex Education," *Planned Parenthood*, https://www.plannedparenthood.org/learn/for-educators.

30. This documentary is primarily about Planned Parenthood's abortion history, but that history dovetails with the sexual revolution and subject of this chapter: *The 1916 Project*, https://the1916project.com/.

31. Lancing and Lindsay, *The Queering of the American Child*, chapter 6.

32. Foundation Worldview, "God's Good Design Curriculum," https://foundationworldview.com/curriculum/gods-good-design.

33. Christopher Yuan, "The Holy Sexuality Project," https://holysexuality.com/.

OTHER GREAT BOOKS
BY NATASHA CRAIN

CULTURAL ISSUES

Faithfully Different

Faithfully Different helps Christians identify and respond to today's most significant pressures on the biblical worldview, including cancel culture, secular social justice, progressive Christianity, deconstruction, virtue signaling, and more.

APOLOGETICS FOR PARENTS

Keeping Your Kids on God's Side

Keeping Your Kids on God's Side introduces parents to 40 of the most important faith challenges facing kids today. It's an easy-to-understand "apologetics 101," covering the subject areas of God, truth and worldviews, Jesus, the Bible, and science.

Talking with Your Kids about God

Talking with Your Kids about God equips parents for 30 must-have conversations with kids about God given the increasingly atheistic culture in which they're growing up.

Talking with Your Kids about Jesus

Talking with Your Kids about Jesus equips parents for 30 must-have conversations with kids about Jesus to prepare them for the challenges they'll encounter to Christianity. Six-session video curriculum available through RightNow Media.

To learn more about Harvest House books and
to read sample chapters, visit our website:

www.HarvestHousePublishers.com

HARVEST HOUSE PUBLISHERS
EUGENE, OREGON